The Court Theatre 1904-1907

Books of the Theatre Series

H. D. Albright, General Editor

Number 6   *December 1966*

A Rare Books of the Theatre project of the
American Educational Theatre Association

DESMOND MacCARTHY'S
The Court Theatre 1904-1907
A Commentary and Criticism

Edited, with a foreword and additional material, by

Stanley Weintraub

UNIVERSITY OF MIAMI PRESS
CORAL GABLES, FLORIDA 33124

Printed in the United States of America
ATLANTIC PRINTERS, MIAMI BEACH, FLORIDA

CONTENTS

FOREWORD

As the 1966 volume in the BOOKS OF THE THEATRE SERIES, the editors are pleased to present a new and enlarged edition of the late Sir Desmond MacCarthy's *The Court Theatre 1904-1907*. The original edition (London, 1907) was a contemporary appraisal of the four famous Vedrenne-Barker seasons at the Royal Court Theatre in Sloane Square, plus an appendix of reprinted programs of each first night. The present reissue is augmented by a transcript of the remarks of noted theatrical personalities on the occasion of a testimonial dinner—i.e., for Vedrenne and Barker when the Royal Court seasons came to a close. There is also a critical introduction by the volume's editor, Stanley Weintraub.

This sixth volume in the series is again a joint undertaking of the University of Miami Press and the Rare Books of the Theatre Project of the American Educational Theatre Association. David G. Schaal has been the Project Chairman.

The Court Theatre allows us to see Shaw against the background of some of his most important contemporaries, including Galsworthy, Hankin, and Granville-Barker, as well as Gilbert Murray, whose new translations of the Greek classics formed a portion of the theatre program. In addition, the book's first chapter is a first-class summary of the Court Theatre's acting and methods of production, written by a discerning contemporary critic. Taken as a whole, the work is a major memorial to a significant era in the English theatre —perhaps, as the editor of the present edition suggests, the most significant since Sheridan's day.

H. D. ALBRIGHT
General Editor

The editors and publishers acknowledge with gratitude the kindness of Mr. Michael MacCarthy in granting permission for British distribution of this volume.

EDITOR'S INTRODUCTION
The Court and the Shavian Revolution

On Easter Monday, 1956, the Royal Court Theatre—a small, shabby playhouse belying its pretentious name—reopened under a new management, The English Stage Company. Actor-director George Devine (1910-1966) was in charge, and the play was a promising new one, novelist Angus Wilson's *The Mulberry Bush*. Reaction from the critics was lukewarm. The not-so-new Arthur Miller drama *The Crucible* was next, and the notices were respectful. The third play on the schedule opened on the eighth of May, a work in a harsh, realistic vein by an unemployed twenty-six-year-old actor, John Osborne. *Look Back in Anger* brought to the hallowed old boards a new generation's iconoclasms, and when the shock waves reached the press and public, it was clear that the event had changed the direction of British drama.

After Osborne there were others—Wesker, Pinter, Arden, Simpson, Dennis, Jellicoe.... And the Royal Court was hospitable, too, to the puzzling and often forbidding new European drama—Ionesco, Brecht, Beckett, Frisch, Genet. Some productions lost money, others sold out their runs; and the influence of the Court again radiated throughout the theatre world. Fifty-two years before *Look Back in Anger*, the twentieth century had come to English drama in the small (it seated only 614) playhouse adjoining Sloane Square station on the Metropolitan District Railway,[1] far from the West End hub of London theatre. Then—as now—an actor-director, and a combination of original English plays and imported offerings by new Continental dramatists, had made the Royal Court

---

[1]Sloane Square Station is now a stop on the Circle Line in the London Transport system.

stage the battleground on which a decisive struggle for a new drama had been fought, and largely won.

It had all begun with no revolution in mind; but the six hesistantly-introduced matinees of *Candida* yielded a small profit, and induced the cautious John E. Vedrenne, then manager of the Court, to join the young actor-director of the Shaw performances, Harley Granville-Barker, in a limited play-producing partnership. Vedrenne's prudence had been undermined as early as the first matinee of *Candida,* on April 26, 1904, when the curtain came down on repeated shouts of "Author!" Vedrenne finally mounted the stage and began a speech. "Ladies and Gentlemen," he explained, "I am not Shaw, who is probably on the platform of the station next door." The theatre emptied hardly before Vedrenne had finished, the audience leaving its seats and hurrying to Sloane Square station to try to catch a glimpse of Shaw.[2]

On October 18, 1904, a season of twenty-seven matinee performances was begun with the production of *The Hippolytus* of Euripides in Gilbert Murray's translation, followed by plays by Bernard Shaw, Maurice Maeterlinck, and Laurence Housman (in collaboration with Barker). Because all the performances were to be in the afternoon, actors could be induced to play in them at a small salary: it left them free to accept evening engagements in the West End. Still, the low overhead of an out-of-the-way theatre and part-time players had to be balanced by the fact that the Court had severely narrowed its potential audience to persons who had their afternoons to spend at leisure.

By the following February the management had decided to take a full lease of the Court and offer a repertory of evening as well as matinee performances. Vedrenne and Barker agreed to take £20 a week as salary—actually an advance on hoped-for box-office receipts—and to spend no more than £200 to mount a production. At first members of the stock company were to be paid £3 a week, a wage which could only have

---

[2]According to Hesketh Pearson's *George Bernard Shaw* (1942), G.B.S. was gone by the time his admirers arrived.

appealed to dedicated artists. And these were. They flowered under the repertory system and the Barker-Shaw discipline, which encouraged creativity and exploited the possibilities of even the smallest roles, developing into satisfying opportunities parts which would have been only afterthoughts under the star system. The scripts contributed, too, for the Shavian philosophy of dramaturgy and direction, transmitted to Barker, was that when actors are asked to learn their lines, they should have lines worth speaking.

From the start Bernard Shaw was heavily involved, and his plays, old and new, were the backbone of the repertory (with one sometimes rushed into revival to replace a foundering drama by another hand). Vedrenne—at thirty-seven, ten years older than Barker—handled the business side of the theatre's affairs, worrying as much about the pence as he did about the pounds, convinced—and sometimes rightly so—that the management daily trod the edge of insolvency. Barker was responsible for the artistic side, but when a Shaw play was produced—as happened in 701 of the 988 performances from 1904 through 1907—G.B.S. was his own director, choosing and rehearsing the cast and advising on related production matters, from music and scene design to props and stage machinery. He even wrote his own program notes, although not under his signature, as when *Man and Superman* was first produced in 1905:

> Messrs. Vedrenne and Barker beg leave to explain that the acting version of *Man and Superman* now presented has been prepared solely by the author. None of the omissions by which he has brought the performance within the customary limits of time have been made or suggested by the managers. They do not regard a complete performance, occupying both afternoon and evening, as impossible or unacceptable. But as Mr. Bernard Shaw designed the play from the beginning so as to admit of the excision, for practical stage purposes, of the scene in which John Tanner's motor-car is stopped in Spain by brigands, of the philosophical episode of Don Juan in

xiii

Hell, and of the disquisition on the evolution of morality as a passion, they feel that they can present the rest of the play as a complete comedy in three acts without injury to the artistic integrity of the work, or violation of the author's wishes, which have been unconditionally complied with on all points.

For the popular Court production Barker was made up for his John Tanner role as a young, auburn-bearded Bernard Shaw, establishing a tradition often followed since, as has been the custom that the aged mariner-prophet Captain Shotover (of *Heartbreak House*, in 1921) suggest the older, white-whiskered G.B.S. Roughly between the initial production of the two plays, Shaw—already forty-eight at the opening of the first Court season—became and remained the idol of a generation of young intellectuals who were excited and challenged by his brand of irreverence and eloquence, vitality and unconventionality. After *Man and Superman* Shaw was so much in demand—as a lecturer as well as a playwright—that he wrote facetiously to his agent to say that his terms to take the platform would be "a million dollars for a tour, not including the salary of Paderewski at the piano."[3]

The first Shaw play to premiere at the Court had been his comedy of Irish and English manners, *John Bull's Other Island*, on November 1, 1904. It was to have played only the standard opening six matinees, but Beatrice Webb brought the Prime Minister, A. J. Balfour, to a performance. Afterwards, newspapers reported that he was so delighted by it that he came a second time with one leader of the Opposition (Campbell-Bannerman) and a third with the other (Asquith). It assured the play's popular success. A Command Performance had to be staged when King Edward VII expressed a desire to see it, for the play by then had completed a second scheduled run. The request must have come as a shock to G.B.S., for Edward, as Prince of Wales, had seen *Arms and the Man* in its 1894 premiere at the Avenue Theatre. While the audience exploded

---

[3]Shaw to Reginald Golding Bright, October 27, 1904, in *Advice to a Young Critic*, ed. E. J. West (New York, 1963), p. 155.

with laughter, he had greeted the farce with studied grimness, once bursting from his box into the uncontaminated air of the corridor to mutter that Shaw "must be mad." "His Royal Highness," a more moderate statement from the Palace afterwards had announced, "regretted that the play should have shown so disrespectful an attitude toward the Army as was betrayed by the character of the chocolate-cream soldier."

Edward's Court Theatre visit put the seal of the Crown upon Shaw's reputation as England's leading playwright, especially when it was learned that—contrary to the previous Royal experience—the King, sitting in the Royal Box in special furniture Vedrenne had rented for the occasion, had laughed so heartily that he had broken his chair. The special performance (on March 11, 1905) gained the producers nothing at the box office, and even set them back the price of an expensive chair, but they carefully offered Shaw the standard royalty for it anyway. Shaw returned the check with a facetious note, pointing out that the performance was an "unauthorized" one, and that if he accepted royalties he would be "compounding a felony." It was not the only time Shaw had declined payment, for when a triple-bill which included his own pot-boiler *How He Lied to Her Husband* flopped (the other two plays were by Yeats and Schnitzler) Shaw wrote to Vedrenne that since his play had proved worthless, in spite of the management's doing its best for it, he would not aggravate its failure by accepting royalties, "which I hereby formally waive, forego and disclaim."

The Command Performance initiated a Shaw boom that the playwright—after enduring a decade of indifference from theatre managers—could only view with scorn. "I do most certainly resent being bothered about productions," he wrote his agent. "These idiots leave me in peace for ten years and then rush for me because the King orders a performance at the Court Theatre. They will make just as great a mess of producing me as they did before of *not* producing me. Put them out. Order them off. Call the police, if necessary. Daly [who had made *Candida* the hit of the New York season in 1904] and Vedrenne-Barker can still have me at 10%: all others 25%."[4]

Relations between the Court's management and its play-wright-almost-in-residence were not always that smooth, although Granville Barker was fast becoming as much surrogate son as disciple to Shaw. Shaw encouraged bigger-than-life acting, while Barker (according to his biographer, C. B. Purdom) sought the "expressive detail" of the early Tom Robertson school of realism. Barker gradually altered his understated approach to accommodate G.B.S., but not enough to keep Shaw from declaring that Barker's style was "as different from mine as Debussy's from Verdi." Possibly Shaw was present at the rehearsal of one of his plays when Barker entreated the cast, "Do remember, ladies and gentle-men, that this is Italian opera."

Although he would often blarney actors and management into doing his will, Shaw could blaze with invective when he thought he saw bad acting or direction, or inept choice of plays. When Louis Calvert played the formidable Undershaft (in *Major Barbara*) badly, Shaw was furious, and told him so, afterwards remarking to Beatrice Webb (who confided it to her diary) that Calvert had "lost his nerve" over the role—that he "could not understand or remember his part and was aghast at what he considered its black immorality." The mere physical filling of a role never satisfied Shaw. After some quibbling over casting a part, he once insisted to Barker, "It is all very well to say there are others. . . . But if you want the higher Shaw drama you must take higher chances." Later, Shaw castigated the casting of Galsworthy's *The Silver Box*, telling Barker and Vedrenne that excellence of direction could not conceal flaws in personnel: "Get your cast right, and get them interested in themselves and in the occasion. . . . Get your cast wrong; and you wreck your play just to the extent to which your cast is wrong. . . . As it was, the stage business was as perfect as a quadrille; but the parts simply did not exist. . . ."

[4]Shaw to Golding Bright, March 8, 1905, in *Advice to a Young Critic*, p. 162.

The *How He Lied* debacle had proved Shaw capable of self-criticism as well as criticism, and at least once afterwards in the Court years, rather than condemn the acting or casting, he blamed his own writing. Ellen Terry had finally succumbed to his entreaties that she play Lady Cecily in six matinees of *Captain Brassbound's Conversion*, a role Shaw had written for her seven years before. In her sixtieth year (and fiftieth as an actress), she was suddenly self-conscious and unsure of herself, disappointingly no longer up to roles which demanded a lightness of touch; and the presence of a great lady of the theatre was not the draw the Court management had hoped.

But Shaw admired Ellen Terry too unreservedly to discredit her performance. "All our real successes," he explained to Vedrenne, ". . . have been with modest and youthful casts"; yet lest this rationalization infer a criticism of Miss Terry, he suggested, evading reference to the Lady Cecily part, that the play was at fault: "For some reason, Drinkwater is not amusing in the first act, and Brassbound is not thrilling in the second." However even at rehearsals, he knew, Miss Terry had been nervously garbling her lines, impelling Vedrenne to ask Shaw concernedly whether she was speaking what Shaw had written. "No," G.B.S. covered for her; "but she's speaking them as I ought to have written them." Nevertheless, it was a lesson learned—although for years Shaw continued to insist, Ellen Terry in mind, that the Lady Cecily role required "artistic faculty and personal attraction of a very rare order." For the first and only time, the Court had succumbed to that despoiler of the repertory principle, star casting.

One of the rare occasions when Shaw did not direct a Court production of his own work was a revival of *You Never Can Tell*, rehearsed by Barker while Shaw was holidaying across the Channel. When Shaw saw the play later in production he found "a degree of infamy which took my breath away," writing to Barker (July 19, 1906), "What was the name of the author of that play?" Yet he ended the letter warmly, "P.S. We can put you up here and give you a room to write in if you would like." When Barker chose plays for matinees which Shaw felt were poor theatre, and below Court standards

—and the box-office take reinforced the impression—Shaw, who wanted the Court to pay and prove its way, talked openly of bankruptcy. But the Court had to take chances in order to try to develop new dramatists, even when six matinees of a thin double bill by novelist Maurice Hewlett took in only £13. Sometimes—when he felt the playwright showed promise (as with a young seaman named John Masefield and his grim, Elizabethan-like tragedy, *The Campden Wonder*)—Shaw applauded the attempt although the play was both a box office and a critical catastrophe. But he complained that Barker had wrecked its chances by double-billing the tragedy to follow a vapid comedy, Cyril Harcourt's *The Reformer*. "The Campden Wonder," G.B.S. prophesied, "in its proper place in a proper bill, can force the public to reverse the press verdict."[5]

There would be no chance to reverse the verdict on Masefield's play, for the final months at the Court followed its production, the management finding the enterprise continuing to be financially precarious (although it actually ended by turning a small profit). Vedrenne and Barker felt that the out-of-the-way location of the Royal Court was the chief factor influencing its shaky economics, and dreamed of transferring operations to the more prestigious West End. Actually, the Court management had created a following where it was, and needed only to cultivate and enlarge it through appropriate choice of a repertory. It had become the first successful attempt to establish a repertory theatre in England, and the patrons of the Court were already, in Shaw's words, "not an audience but a congregation." Neither Vedrenne nor Barker, Shaw wrote them, understood "what has made the Court possible. I have given you a series of first-rate music-hall entertainments, thinly disguised as plays, but really offering the public a unique string of turns by comics and serio-comics of every popular type. . . . Make no error V.D. that is the jam that has carried the propaganda pill down [and] . . . consoled

---

[5]Masefield had first shown up at the Court to whistle some sea chanty tunes to Barker, who was thinking of using sea chanties in the second act of a revival of Shaw's *Captain Brassbound's Conversion*. Masefield had composed them himself while serving on an ancient wooden sailing ship.

the house for the super drama." It was not geography, but erratic choice of plays, he thought, which now and then had brought them close to red ink. "Why," he asked, "do you deliberately choose the worse play, the less popular play, the stale play. . . ?"[6]

The Vedrenne-Barker seasons at the Court ended in the glow of three concluding successes, revivals of Barker's (and Laurence Housman's) popular fantasy *Prunella*, Shaw's *Man and Superman*, and a final double bill of Shaw's *Man of Destiny* and the dream interlude from *Superman*, *Don Juan in Hell*, in its first performances. (The *Don Juan* was a brilliantly staged and acted production, the four-character play so sumptuously costumed by Charles Ricketts that Vedrenne worried that the clothing bill would cause him to conclude the three years at the Court in debt.) On July 7, a week after the season ended, a testimonial dinner attended by leading figures in the London theatrical world honored the Vedrenne-Barker management.[7] It was the crown upon the Royal Court's efforts. Even the shadowy Vedrenne was there, Charles Ricketts quipping to Shaw afterwards that he had gone to the dinner "to find out, incidentally, if Vedrenne really existed: like all men, I had viewed him as merely a smart impersonation of Barker's done with a wig and a pair of blue spectacles."[8]

Sweetness and light pervaded most of the evening, but Barker made an uncomplimentary remark about the impact of actor-managers on the drama in the presence of the expansively gracious actor-manager Beerbohm Tree, and Shaw, interrupting a display of witty pyrotechnics, lashed out at the Press, "which from first to last has done what in it lay to crush the enterprise. . . . There you will find a chronicle of failure, a sulky protest against this new and troublesome sort of entertainment that calls for knowledge and thought instead of

---

[6]Yet Shaw only three months afterward (July 27, 1907) would offer to back their Savoy Theatre venture to the tune of £2000. Obviously, he found some saving merit in the Court system and management.

[7]For complete texts of all the speakers' remarks at the dinner, see Appendix II.

[8]C. B. Purdom, *Harley Granville Barker* (Cambridge, Mass., 1956), p. 65.

the usual cliches." The attack was too sweeping, for there were now at least an influential minority of drama critics sympathetic to change, like Desmond MacCarthy, whose criticism (particularly of Shaw) remains one of the best bodies of analytical writing on the Edwardian drama.[9]

There was also, almost in spite of himself, *The Times*'s A. B. Walkley, who shuddered as the gusts of change buffeted him in his seat on the aisle, and refused to admit that such Court offerings as *Man and Superman*—the published version of which G.B.S. had dedicated to him—were plays at all. (Admittedly, they were scintillating intellectual entertainments, but improperly called dramas.) Yet Walkley found himself praising Barker as a "born interpreter of his talent," writing of the ensemble playing of the Court company, including its Shaw performances, "There is no such all-round acting in London as is nowadays to be seen at the Court Theatre. . . . Where all are excellent it is needless to single out names." There was also Shaw's other faint-praising old journalistic friend from the Eighties, the *Tribune*'s William Archer, who doggedly considered Pinero a dramatic genius and Shaw— whom he vainly strove to convert to Pineroticism—"clever rather than convincing." Even so, Archer, while temperamentally at odds with the Court's general choice of plays, was temporarily won over by *John Bull's Other Island* ("One of the richest pieces of comedy of modern times"). Archer celebrated the Court's first year by publishing *A Record and a Commentary of the Vedrenne-Barker Season, 1904-1905* (London, 1906), the model for MacCarthy's later, more comprehensive account.

Of more importance to the Shavian revolution than Archer or Walkley was Beerbohm Tree's half-brother, Max Beerbohm

---

[9]MacCarthy, later Sir Desmond (1878-1952), began to write on the theatre in 1904, the year of the first Court season, when he joined the staff of *The Speaker*. In 1913 he moved (as "Affable Hawk") to *The New Statesman*—just in time to do memorable reviews of the first English productions of Shaw's *Androcles and the Lion* and Chekhov's *Uncle Vanya*. Later he succeeded Sir Edmund Gosse as the leading critic of the London *Sunday Times*. A member of the famous Bloomsbury circle, he was a friend of Leonard and Virginia Woolf, Clive and Vanessa Bell, Roger Fry, E. M. Foster, Lytton Strachey, and John Maynard Keynes. Virginia Woolf drew him as Bernard in her novel *The Years*.

who from his *Saturday Review* critic's chair (to which he had
succeeded Shaw in 1898) wrote understandingly of the new
dramatists of the Court. Max's reviews of the plays of Barker,
Hankin, and Galsworthy must have encouraged even Vedrenne.[10] More significantly, Max's Royal Court reviews of
G.B.S. demonstrated the progress of a skeptical intelligence
toward awareness of Shaw's aims and methods. Before the
Court seasons he had seen Shaw in less effective productions,
and reviewed the unproduced plays from the published edi-
tions, often coming to the standard contemporary opinion that
a Shaw play was little more than a tract set in type in something resembling play form. In print, *Man and Superman* had
seemed to him a "peculiar article" and "not a play at all. It
is 'as good as a play'—infinitely better . . . than any play I
have ever read or seen enacted. But a play it is not." Shaw,
he concluded, "Having no sense for life," had "necessarily,
no sense for art." (Sept. 12, 1903).

Then, on a cold November afternoon, in the drafty Royal
Court, remote from his usual West End haunts, he sat through
a matinee of *John Bull's Other Island*, and experienced the
first of what would be a series of revelations:

> . . . In a warm theatre, within the regular radius
> for theatres, after nightfall—in fact with just those
> cheerful commercial circumstances which are with-
> held from them—these plays would soon take the
> town. . . .
>
> The critics . . . have raised their usual parrot-cry:
> "Not a play." This, being interpreted, means "Not a
> love-story, split neatly up into four brief acts. . . . Not
> much actually happens in the play. The greater part
> of the play is talk: and the talk is often not relevant
> to the action, but merely to the characters, and to
> things in general. Pray, why is this not to be called a

---

[10]Beerbohm published a selection of his critiques for *The Saturday Review* from 1898 through 1910 as *Around Theatres* (1924 and other re-
printings since).

play? Why should the modern "tightness" of technique[11] be regarded as a sacred and essential part of dramaturgy? And why should the passion of love be regarded as the one possible theme in dramaturgy? Between these two superstitions lies the main secret of the barrenness of modern English drama. The first of them wards away the majority of men of creative literary power.... The second prevents playwrights from taking themes which would both invigorate their work through novelty and bring the theatre into contact with life at large. (November 12, 1904)

It was obvious, then, from the first review of a Court-produced Shaw play signed "Max" that the Shavian revolution had begun to succeed. That its success was assured was proven thirteen months later, when Beerbohm, fresh from viewing the Court production of *Man and Superman*, attended the opening of *Major Barbara*. Rather than merely surveying the performance, he reviewed his, and other reviewers', past critical positions regarding the Shavian drama—that G.B.S. could not draw flesh-and-blood characters, that his *dramatis personae* were only Shaws in trousers or petticoats, that his so-called plays were devoid of the substance of drama. Max saw the Court premiere of *Major Barbara* attacked in this fashion not only as a non-play, but because of the Salvation Army setting of its second act, and some attendant religious references in the dialogue, as a piece of arrogant and tasteless sacrilege. Walkley even had concluded, sadly, that it was useless to argue with Shaw "over these things. He will do them. All we can do is be sorry." (Actually, Shaw had the delighted co-operation of the Army, which lent uniforms and technical advice, and welcomed Shaw's sympathetic disagreement with its philosophy as good advertising. Some Salvation Army officials even had a box for the opening, although the Army usually discouraged theatre attendance as sinful.) The act in question, Max observed, included characters who "live with

---

[11]Apparently a reference to the "well-made" play of the Scribe-Sardou school ("Sardoodledom" to Shaw), popularly represented in England by the tightly-plotted society melodramas of Pinero.

an intense vitality," was "as cunning a piece of craftsmanship as any conventional playwright could achieve," and had "a cumulative appeal to the emotions which no other living playwright has touched."

Yet Max wrote of those of his colleagues still fighting a rear-guard action against the twentieth century: "With all these facts staring them in the face, they still maintain that Mr. Shaw is not a playwright." But Max, at least, had "climbed down." "That theory might have held water in the days before Mr. Shaw's plays were acted. Indeed," he confessed, "I was in the habit of propounding it myself. . . . This simply proved that I had not enough theatrical imagination to see the potentialities of a play when reading it in print. . . ." Still, he had to admit, the "old superstition" had lingered, and he felt the need to recant his earlier remarks that plays like *Man and Superman* were "quite unsuited to any stage." After he had seen it done at the Court, he had changed his mind; and the Court's *Major Barbara* reinforced his feeling that it was "both unjust and absurd" to deny that Shaw was a dramatist of the first importance "merely because he chooses, for the most part, to get the drama out of contrasted types of character and thought, without action, and without appeal to the emotions. . . . His technique is peculiar because his purpose is peculiar. . . ."

The Royal Court would make the new techniques, and the existence of serious purpose in the drama, less "peculiar," and Shaw's testimonial dinner blast at the critics who still wore blinders was not a rationalization of failure. New dramatists had ventured out onto the Court's stage; a new theatre audience had been created and cultivated; and acting, production, and playwriting had left the nineteenth century and entered the twentieth. Many of the Royal Court company would have long and distinguished stage careers, one at least (Sir Lewis Casson) continuing for sixty years after his debut at the Court. Continental playwrights like Maeterlinck, Schnitzler, and Hauptmann were introduced to the English public; and classical Greek drama through the example of the verse translations of Gilbert Murray was proven viable for the modern stage. Some of the new English dramatists proved disappointing, and Shaw tried to lure other writers via the Court's hospitable example—Wells, Conrad, Chesterton, Kipling—to try playwriting. Still, there were successes. A novelist named John Galsworthy would afterwards give as much time to the drama as to fiction. Laurence Housman would continue to write plays, and John Masefield would produce a long series of verse dramas.

Two writers who raised the greatest expectations failed to realize them. St. John Hankin died at thirty-nine, a few years after his promising work at the Court; and Granville Barker himself was prevented by a combination of circumstances from fulfilling the potential of his Court plays. His *The Voysey Inheritance*, staged at the Court in November, 1905, was called by Walkley *"triple extrait de Shaw"* because of its apparent spare emotional content and sardonic irony, and its willingness to question the assumptions upon which the lives of its audiences were based. But Barker, who had great gifts in characterization, although not strong on theatrical construction, ran into trouble with the Lord Chamberlain's censorship with his next play, *Waste*. (A political drama, it was refused a license when the playwright declined to cut references to, among other things, an abortion.) Afterwards he wrote only one other play which reached the stage, *The Madras House*, a dryly intellectual study of sexual attitudes in Edwardian England. After the First World War he ceased regular play producing, and wrote little but Shakespearian criticism.[12] Two later plays were never performed, and his reputation emerges from the shadows primarily with reference to the years at the Royal Court.

Although the commercial theatre could seem to remain grandly aloof from the influences of the Court, distant as were Shaftesbury Avenue and the Strand both geographically

---

[12]His partner at the Court and later ventures, Vedrenne, worked with him until March, 1911, when the management ended in debt—and G.B.S. underwrote the losses. Vedrenne continued in theatre management, making a fortune in a partnership which produced the Arnold Bennett-Edward Knoblock long-running *Milestones* (1912). He died in 1930, sixteen years before Barker.

and metaphorically, they were changing under pressure. For one thing, the Court performances had created intense West End interest in the previously untouchable Shaw. Other Court playwrights, like Galsworthy, could find stages for their later plays, while playwrights like Maugham could add Royal Court honesty of dialogue and theme to the post-Wildean comedies of manners. There was fresh interest in previously unfashionable dramatists from abroad, even those who violated previously sacrosanct Edwardian reticences and taboos. Other theatres and playwrights could follow, and offer in commercial terms what was only achieved earlier with frustrating difficulty.

That the Royal Court did not enrich its management was no clue to its success or failure. The very fact of an important book published immediately after the event to both celebrate and elucidate it—Desmond MacCarthy's *The Court Theatre*— is indication of the significance with which Vedrenne and Barker's contemporaries accepted the experiment.[13] Shaw later described his reaction to the need he had seen then for a new perspective toward the theatre (he was actually referring to one of his plays first staged at the Court):

I did not cut these cerebral capers in mere inconsiderate exuberance. I did it because the worst convention of the criticism of the theatre current at that time was that intellectual seriousness is out of place on the stage; that the theatre is a place of shallow amusement; that people go there to be soothed after the enormous intellectual strain of a day in the city: in short, that a playwright is a person whose business it is to make unwholesome confectionery out of cheap emotions. My answer to this was to put all my intellectual goods in the shop window under the sign of Man and Superman. That part of my design suc-

---

[13]Perhaps Archer's more preliminary tribute, *A Record and a Commentary of the Vedrenne Barker Season, 1904-1905*, was of more *immediate* significance, for it was a bow in the direction of the "new" theatre from a critic who generally saw the wave of the future elsewhere. It remains a more limited work.

ceeded. By good luck and acting, the comedy triumphed on the stage; and the book was a good deal discussed. Since then the sweet-shop view of the theatre has been out of countenance. . . . And the younger playwrights are not only taking their art seriously, but being taken seriously themselves. . . .[14]

The chronicle of the Royal Court is the record of the first major twentieth-century attempt to have the English theatre and its audience take themselves seriously.

STANLEY WEINTRAUB

---

[14]Preface to *Back to Methuselah*, 1921.

DESMOND MacCARTHY'S
The Court Theatre 1904-1907

Edited by Stanley Weintraub

INTRODUCTION

The Influence of Dramatic Criticism

IT may sometimes depress the critic to reflect how little
influence he has upon the fate of the plays and books he
criticizes, but this fact is the salvation of criticism, and often,
let me hasten to add, the salvation of art. If the case were
otherwise, and the critic knew his opinion had a direct effect
upon the commercial success of a play, he could hardly bring
himself to point out carefully the defects of a performance,
which he thought, nevertheless, far better than its competitors
for public favour. He would feel bound, in such a case, to
consider the immediate effect of what he wrote, and this pre-
occupation would be fatal to criticism. Happily, we need
not think of this. It is obvious that success is achieved inde-
pendently of the opinion of critics; the sky is red with spread-
ing, blazing reputations which their cold water is as powerless
to quench as a fire-engine a prairie fire; nor can their unani-
mous praise always secure even a modicum of success. For
instance, in March 1905, the Court Theatre Company produced
a translation of Hauptmann's *Bieber Pelz*, called *The Thieves'
Comedy*. It was a first-rate performance, and an exceptionally
good play. The critics praised it with one accord; not only
those who had begun to see in the Vedrenne-Barker management the most notable achievement in modern dramatic production, but also those who were reluctant to admit anything
of the kind. They praised the acting, the play, the point; they
lavished on it those adjectives which are calculated to rouse
curiosity; but the play ran out after nine performances before
almost empty houses. It is not likely, in the event of its revival,
that it would again fall flat; but that would be due to Messrs.
Vedrenne and Barker having now gained the confidence of a
considerable public, in securing which the support of even the
most authoritative critics has only played an ancillary part.

If, then, the public do not follow the critics, why do they read them? That they do so is certain, since every daily and weekly paper continues to provide criticism in large quantities.

Dramatic criticism finds two kinds of readers; those who just glance at the plot and the names of the "stars" to discover whether a play is likely to amuse them, and those who, equally or even more anxious to discover this, are interested at the same time in discussions upon the merits and meanings of plays. To the former, dramatic criticism is simply a species of elaborated, garbled news, less trustworthy than a hint from an acquaintance; to the others it is an expression of opinion upon topics which they are in the habit of discussing themselves. If a critic is interesting they read him, but with no more subservience than they would feel towards a writer who was not a critic: the direct influence of criticism is therefore, in either case, likely to be small. Judging, however, from the prodigious quantity of talk exchanged over plays and novels, readers of the latter kind are numerous enough; even allowing for the fact that conversation upon art and literature is one of the commonest masks that politeness finds for boredom. In France this fact is recognized, and interest at the back of all this general talk about the drama finds a better continuation in the Press. French dramatic critics are allowed at least twenty-four hours during which to examine and express their impressions, while our daily-paper critics are hustled into print an hour or two after leaving the theatre. It is they who are most widely read, while it is their work which is perforce most carelessly done. The deft and spirited *Times* may plunge into his subject at any point, and in a few energetic sentences reach the centre of his theme; but a combination of endowments including logic, quickness, and a fly-paper memory, which catches every telling phrase, is as rare as it is essential under such conditions. On the other hand, a critic may be capable of gathering a fair harvest of observation, without having the high-pressure mental machinery to reap and thresh it within a couple of hours, and such critics have now no chance of doing their best. Consequently they are in disgrace in all quarters: managers talk as though they would gladly be rid of them; actors are sick of finding their acting dismissed in a few vague phrases at the end of an account of the plot, their strokes of imagination unnoticed, their bungling carelessly praised; authors complain that their plays are misunderstood—Mr. Shaw frequently writes prefaces to show they are dunder-heads; their editors cut them down, their readers think they could do better themselves. All this would surprise nobody who had seen a first-night rush back to newspaper offices, where copy is often snatched away in the writing, and the time allowed commonly varies from forty to a hundred minutes. So driven, a man will usually find himself writing, not what he would most like to express, but whatever he can put down quickest. The remedy is simple: the editors must be persuaded to accept a brief "report" of the first night and to hold over the critical account of the play till the following issue; or, better still, for a weekly *feuilleton*. It would pay them well: they would be getting far better copy; they would please a section of the public they never cease to cater for by literary articles and reviews of all kinds, while they would be providing the people, who choose their plays by rules of thumb, just the prompt, ungarnished news they require on the following morning. That it would be an advantage, from the point of view of the theatres, if critics were enabled to write their best, may seem in contradiction with the fact that criticism has little direct influence; for it is certainly true that the sale of tickets depends upon the taste of the public, and not upon the taste of the critic; but criticism has nevertheless a strong indirect influence: an example can be taken from the history of the Court Theatre.

In accounting for its success, after you have pointed to the originality and power of Mr. Shaw's plays and the intelligence and naturalness of the acting, further explanations may seem as superfluous as Harlequin's thirty-six reasons why his dead master could not appear; yet if we do seek further, the influence of ten years' criticism upon public sentiment, during which the most entertaining critics assaulted the stock London play, laughed at its hackneyed situations, its vapid sentiments, exposed its reach-me-down solutions and superficial problems, must be taken into consideration in accounting for the difference between the success of Messrs. Vedrenne and Barker and that of such intermittent enterprises, so similar in spirit, as the Independent and New Century Theatres.

Beside the comparatively few people who knew all along what they wanted from the theatre, there were a large number who knew vaguely what they did *not* want, but were inclined to explain their constant dissatisfaction by telling themselves that they were not naturally fond of the drama. The few who knew what they wanted went to the Independent and New Century Theatres, or joined the Stage Society; the others, without being convinced completely, began to be persuaded, by such critics as "G. B. S.," "Max," Mr. William Archer and Mr. Walkley, that there might be the best reasons for their lack of interest in the average play. When in 1904 the Court Theatre started under a new management, the enterprise this time did not wear the truculent, propagandist aspect of the Independent Theatre; Ibsen was no longer a bugbear, though he was far from being a draw; the plays of Mr. Shaw had been widely read, and there was considerable curiosity to see them; *Arms and the Man* and the few performances already given of *You Never Can Tell, The Devil's Disciple,* and *Candida* had been remembered and talked about; and, moreover, Messrs. Vedrenne and Barker had the good fortune to produce, as their second play, *John Bull's Other Island,* which attracted all sorts and conditions of men. Society, on the eve of a general election, came to laugh at Broadbent, and to listen to brilliant discussions upon Irish and English character. They sat enthralled through a play with no vestige of a plot, delighted by acting unlit by the light of "a star," which was obviously and incomparably the better for that. Here, too, they found a play the roots of which struck among the interests of the time, which presented types of character delightfully recognizable, yet new to the stage, in which a most natural sequence of events carried them along like a series of ingeniously contrived surprises, and left them with plenty to think over, laugh over, and dispute over when the curtain fell; in short, here was a new play full of qualities which the critics had been arraigning the London stage for not possessing. No wonder when the question of going to

6 •

the theatre next came up people should ask themselves what was being done at the Court.

Thus in an indirect way these critics, who were so amusing to read, had prepared the public to see the significance of the new management; and though it cannot be supposed that were this suggestion, for giving the majority of critics more time, taken up, the result would be a rich crop of remarkable criticisms, certainly the discussions upon the merits and defects of plays would be henceforward much closer, and the articles proportionately more interesting to numbers of people. It is of small consequence that a critic should damn a good play; but it is of consequence that the feeling which criticism promotes should be that plays are well worth discriminating upon, since only in such an atmosphere can drama flourish. Criticism may miss the point again and again; but provided it is of the kind which stimulates impartial scrutiny and interest in the minds of those who concern themselves with works of art, it has fulfilled its main function both as regards art and the public.

THE COURT THEATRE
1904-1907

TOUCHSTONE. Wast ever at the Court, shepherd?
CORIN. No, truly.
TOUCHSTONE. Then thou art damned.

As You Like It, Act III, sc. 2.

CHAPTER I

The Court Theatre

IN 1904 the Court Theatre was in the hands of Mr. J. H. Leigh, who at the time was giving a series of Shakespeare revivals. Mr. Vedrenne was his manager. In February of the same year Mr. Granville Barker, who had produced several plays for the Stage Society, was asked to superintend the production of *The Two Gentlemen of Verona*. He undertook to do this on condition that Mr. Vedrenne would join with him in giving six matinée performances of *Candida*. The proposal was readily accepted, and out of it grew the permanent alliance between them, which has had such important results.

The closest parallel to this joint enterprise is, perhaps, the starting of the Théâtre Libre, in Paris, by M. Antoine, in 1887. In their aims, in their immediate influence upon the drama, and in their successes, these two enterprises have had much in common, though their beginnings were different. M. Antoine began acting before small audiences of subscribers, who were either scoffers or enthusiasts, plays which only ran for three nights; the Passage de l'Elysée des Beaux Arts, where they were performed, was a mean-looking little alley, with nothing propitious about it except its sounding name; in fact, the only advantage that M. Antoine had at the start was his freedom from the censor's interference. The points of resemblance between the two enterprises are that both succeeded in getting the public to appreciate a more natural style of acting, that both were practical protests against the tyranny of the "well-constructed play," that both produced their plays for short runs, and, lastly, that both very quickly collected round them a new school of young playwrights. In each case the same principle lay at the back of their successes and their influence; namely, a determination to get away from what was artificial and theatrical in methods and traditions, and to get back to actuality in gesture, diction, and sentiment. M. Antoine, however, had the more rigid tradition to contend against; Mr. Barker's way had been smoothed by the Independent and New Century theatres, and by the Stage Society. His public was familiar with Ibsen's theory of the stage as a room with a wall knocked in to allow the spectators a view of the interior; while the French public laughed whenever M. Antoine turned his back on the audience.

At the Court the acting pleased from the first. People began to say that the English could act after all, and that London must be full of intelligent actors, of whom nobody had ever heard. Yet, strange to say, these actors, when they appeared in other plays on other boards, seemed to sink again to normal insignificance. The truth was that the Court Theatre acting, which was so much admired and talked about, was only a part of a general theory of dramatic production, which was carried out at every point with the most stringent consistency.

The aim of the management throughout was truth as opposed to effect. The ideas which regulated every detail, decided the importance of each scene and the prominence of each character was a recognition of the truth that in order to make others feel you must feel yourself, and to feel yourself you must be *natural*. This not only implied that actors had to be carefully chosen to fill parts which they could sympathize with and understand, but that every speech, dialogue, and scene had to undergo beforehand the criticism of rigorous common-sense; in fact that the whole play had to be tugged at and tested in rehearsal until the coherence of its idea and the soundness of its sentiment were perfectly established. Now that is not the usual process of production; what happens in the majority of cases is rather this. A prominent actor takes a fancy to a play, because it contains a part which promises him opportunities for bringing off some of his most celebrated effects. He may be aware that there are very weak passages in it; he may feel even in his own part the ground quaking under him at every step; but he knows that his manner is inimitable in a certain scene—say, one in which he pardons an erring woman,—and he relies on his manner, his peculiar knack, or his personal magnetism to carry it off and prevent the audience from feeling the flimsiness of the sentiment or the improbability of the situation.

But the weak places are still there, although the principal scene may be safe in the hands of the "star," and the problem of the producers becomes, how to disguise them as much as possible. I am not discussing here the inevitable consequence of the actor-manager system, which compels the leading actor, who knows that he is the principal attraction, to make his part as prominent as possible and everything lead up to his scenes, even to the detriment of the whole play; but a method of production which affects not only the proportions of the parts, but the manner of acting them. This method is the one of disguising sham sentiment and incongruous utterances by teaching the actors to "carry them off"; so that the art of acting becomes in many cases the art, not of reproducing emotions, but of behaving in such a way that the audience is astonished into not noticing whether the acting is good or bad, or whether the emotion expressed is true or false. The practice of the Court Theatre management has been exactly the reverse of this. The players have been trained *not* to "act" in this sense. The surprisingly good quality of the acting has been mainly due to the fact that the producers have taken pains to see that the actors should have nothing inane or affected set them to say and do; and that the parts should be capable of being acted well, that is to say, naturally and sincerely, from beginning to end. Imagine the predicament of an intelligent actor, who is trying to make a human being out of his part, when he finds that he has to "carry off" some scene or speech which has no vital connection with the character he represents! He must go through with it, he must give it an artificial lift of some kind or other; yet, in doing so, he must make nonsense of the character his art has constructed by means of a hundred little touches of imagination. If you make a man knock the bottom out of his own work in this way, of course he ceases to put his heart and imagination into it. So the main cause of stockishness and lack of imagination among actors is, in the end, the lack of any critical interest in the managers themselves. They have no artistic faith; they are interested, not in human nature, but in dramatic effects; they prefer plays with "show power"; and in consequence they are obliged to train their actors and themselves so as to disguise the weaknesses of such plays, and to avoid natural acting for fear of challenging in the spectator a standard of reality.

Another point with regard to the Court Theatre performances which was quickly noticed was the excellence with which the minor parts were performed. Every actor apparently was willing to accept the smallest part, however marked his success in longer parts might have been. It was worth his while to do this because the producers were careful to leave as much room for him in his scene as the construction of the play allowed. They were absolutely unhampered by either the desire or by the obligation of the actor-manager to make the interest of a performance centre upon one or two characters; with the result that the Court Theatre has been practically the only theatre where it has been worth an actor's while to play a small part, and where the playwright's intentions have been absolutely respected. To take one of many examples. Mr. Edmund Gwenn had made a hit as Straker in *Man and Superman;* when next he appeared he was Baines, the butler, in *The Return of the Prodigal.* He had very few words to say, and he was only on the stage for a few minutes. They were not minutes which were crucial to the development of the story, but they were made important by his imaginative acting. The principal figure, the Prodigal himself (Mr. Matthews), was his interlocutor; but nevertheless as long as Baines was on the stage he was the centre of interest. Not because he out-acted Mr. Matthews, but because his remarks were, at the moment, the most important means towards creating the atmosphere which the author had intended to produce.

About eleven o'clock, the morning after the fainting Prodigal has been found on the door-step, Baines, while clearing away his late, lazy breakfast, begins to discuss with effusive, yet duly respectful interest, his young master's narrow escape from perishing the night before. The Prodigal, whose fainting was a ruse to secure a warmer welcome, naturally discourages an interest in his dramatic return home, and proceeds to ask a string of questions about his industrious and blameless brother and his father's parliamentary prospects. The answers enable him to see how the land lies; but the dialogue was made interesting by the butler's manner, which became at once discreetly and regretfully self-effaced, when he received no encouragement to be sympathetic. Mr. Michael Sherbrooke's Marzo in *Captain Brassbound's Conversion* was an instance of perfect success in a small part, though, unlike the former, not an example of the actor's art of creating a character from a mere hint of the author. He had not a half-dozen lines to speak, yet by becoming so perfectly the childlike Italian rapscallion, he diffused reality all round him, and by his desperate interruption, when Lady Cecily in the trial scene is referred to as a lady—"She no lady. No lady nurse dam rascal. Only saint. She saint"—he drove home the romance of her practical, universal kindness as effectively as Miss Ellen Terry's voice and sweet good-natured manner in the leading part. When will the other London managers learn that the dramatist who is worth his salt needs the co-operation of every part, however small, in order to drive his meaning home; that we want to see plays, not to have our attention riveted perpetually on the same personality for three hours at a stretch? Besides, it is largely by seeing the effect of a personality on others that we come to feel its force, and if the other characters on the stage with the principal figure are not felt to be real people, this reflection of him in their behaviour must be vague and unreal. A leading actor, who is to impress us, must be surrounded by other actors in their way equally convincing; otherwise all we gather from the performance is that he knows his business better than his cast, which as often as not is a poor compliment, and not worth paying half-a-crown to verify.

There is another point which London managers persistently overlook, that good acting can make poor scenery seem real, but that real scenery cannot do the same for poor acting. The Court Theatre had no spare money to lavish on the setting; but who missed the luxurious drawing-room interiors, the silver inkstands on the writing-tables, or the solid bookshelves filled with indubitable books? As every reader of novels knows, if once the novelist has made his heroine speak rightly he can spare a description of her beauty; if he can transmit the emotion of the moment he need only say the sun was up, for his figures to stand in the glances of the morning and the birds to begin to sing in the woods: it is the same with acting and stage properties. Lady Macbeth may drink to the health of her assembling guests from a gilded marmalade pot, if only she raises it properly to her lips, with as much effect as if she drank from a cup copied from a museum treasure.

Sometimes pictorial beauty, however, does help to enforce the sentiment of a scene; but as a rule the simplest means, harmony of colours and agreeable lights and shadows, do this best. When the scene is a strange one it may be necessary to vivify the imagination through the eye, or, in a poetic play, to stir by sights and sounds a contemplative mood in the spectator. The old theory of scenic presentation was to aim at broad effects. This has been supplemented by the practice of crowding the stage with every conceivable property of the most realistic and costly description; but any one who saw the Japanese players when they were here six years ago, or the performance of *Salome*, given by the Literary Theatre Club last summer, or *Don Juan in Hell* at the Court Theatre a few months ago, will feel that a few well-chosen details go further to create a scene than all the usual resources of lavish London management. Moreover, the atmosphere created by the suggestion of a few details, beautiful in themselves, harmonizes more subtly with that which the words create as the play proceeds. Elaborate scenery, however splendid, is, and must remain, a portentous matter of fact; while a scene which is suggested takes significance from all that happens, for it is formed itself out of the spectator's imagination. Scenery of this kind is therefore the only proper setting for a poetic play. In the revivals of Euripides at the

Court Theatre, hardly enough attention was paid to setting of this kind. In the *Hippolytus* the stage was hardly worth looking at; though in the *Electra* the log hut, seen in the cool dusk of morning, with the cypresses standing round it like black candle flames and glimpses of sky beyond and between them, did induce a mood of grave expectancy, befitting the play which was to follow.

These revivals of the Greek drama have been a very important part of the Court Theatre programme. Next to Mr. Shaw with eleven plays comes Euripides with three, on the list of their achievements. As a chronicler and commentator upon the remarkable work of these two and a-half years, I am at a disadvantage in dealing with these Greek plays, having missed the performance of *The Trojan Women*, which was thought far the most impressive of the three. People still talk of Miss Gertrude Kingston's Helen as a piece of acting to treasure in the memory; and readers of the play who considered it contained a too great monotony of sorrow to be effective on the stage, found themselves, to their astonishment, almost unendurably moved. There are no scenes in the Elizabethan drama more terrible than this play itself; there is nothing to equal it for prolonged tragic suffering, for bitterest pathos, or for the sense it inspires of the cruelty of men.

The heroes of Troy are dead when the curtain rises, and their wives are at the mercy of their conquerors and about to be borne away as slaves and concubines. They weep for their children torn from them, for their dead husbands, and for the terrible fate before them; their lamentations are addressed to each other or to the faithless gods, and over all hangs the sense of an implacable fate.

Andromache's last remaining son is taken from her and killed, for fear he should grow up to be the avenger of his house; Helen is delivered over to Menelaus that he may glut his revenge upon her. She is the only one of these women who shows no loyalty or true dignity under calamity. She lies to her husband, saying that she left him against her will, and meets him with ironic effrontery, confident in the power of her radiant charms—well justified indeed, for he takes her home.

The play was performed, in the opinion of the discriminating, with a dignity which made the prolonged exhibition of such sufferings tolerable and beautiful.

In the performance of the *Hippolytus* Mr. Granville Barker's delivery of the messenger's speech was the most memorable feature; in the *Electra,* the spirit in which Miss Wynne-Matthison acted the half-selfless, half-personal passion of Electra herself, and the gravity and beauty of Mr. Lewis Casson's delivery of Castor's speech at the end of the play.

It will be well to state, before going any further, what the aim of the Court Theatre management has been in reviving these Greek plays. Mr. Gilbert Murray's rare and beautiful translations of Euripides proved that, in the hands of a poet and a scholar, the old Greek dramas could be refashioned into plays, which the English reader might enjoy and understand with the same close, effortless sympathy with which he might follow the work of a modern imagination. The performances at the Court Theatre were attempts to carry this feat of transfusion one step further; Mr. Murray had turned Euripides into an English poet-dramatist; Messrs. Vedrenne and Barker tried what could be done towards naturalizing him on the English stage.

Now there are three courses open to those who would present revivals of ancient drama.

One method of success lies in keeping the modern spectator conscious all the time that what he is looking at requires, if it is to be understood and appreciated, a change in his ordinary ways of feeling and judging. The actors, in this case, must aim at archaic dignity; they must stand, move, and speak in such a way that the spectator is perpetually conscious that the effect sought is different from the impression which modern drama would seek to create in such a scene. This is the safest method; it is, too, the simplest by which actors can be got to efface their own personalities, so important a condition in the conveyance of simple and tragic emotions.

The second method, one more tempting and more ambitious, is to supplement the conventions of the ancient stage, which now leave us cold, with modern means of rousing emotion. The Greek Chorus is a convention emotionally unintelligible to us; this second method would add to the utterances of the Chorus the majestic harmonies of tragedy and the music of fear and hope. What a splendid opportunity there is for a triumphant burst from the Chorus at the close of the recognition between Electra and Orestes, one of the most passionate meetings in all drama, or when they rejoice over the death of Ægistheus! With music the Chorus would become to us what it was to the Greeks, a sounding-board to emotion and a means of increasing the spectators' sympathy with what was happening on the stage.

But the Court Theatre chose the third and most difficult method; that of acting the plays as though they had been written for the modern stage. They had no wish to succeed in an æsthetically archaic performance or in an archæologically sentimental revival, and, on the other hand, the introduction of music, by drowning the words, would have hindered their main object, which was to deliver the whole play as it is across the foot-lights. Euripides is so much in sympathy with our way of feeling character and emotion, that it is particularly tempting to bring out the significance of the situations and dialogue by acting them with modern expressiveness. But supposing the managers right in their choice, their treatment of the chorus was very damaging to these plays. On the French stage they have, in some similar revivals, reduced the Chorus to a rudiment, to two venerable old men, one each side of the stage, repeating their speeches alternately. This was very unsatisfactory, but it is doubtful whether it could be more unsatisfactory than the Chorus at the Court. There it was represented by seven or eight ladies, who moved about with slow, elaborate caution, posed like *tableaux vivants*, and uttered the most various sentiments in a monotonous and lugubrious chant, tapering into dismal contralto notes, and conveying no definite emotion, beyond suggesting the earnest desire of the performers themselves to do their best. These lilting sounds were so unfamiliar and mournful, that an *allegro* movement took no effect. The chorus was started off by the leader touching a chord upon a harp, and when she had to speak by herself she always spoke in this artificial manner, even when what she said should have come like a cry from a spectator moved beyond control by sympathy or suspense. For instance, before Electra has recognized her brother, when the chorus is almost certain it is he, the leader exclaims, "O, never was the heart of hopes so hot within me," or, after the murder of Clytemnestra, when brother and sister are overcome with horror at what they have done, she calls out, "Dire is the grief ye have wrought:" these words should sound like excited cries from a spectator deeply stirred, and never spoken in a voice artificially pitched. For whether the Chorus is the "ideal spectator," or whether they belong more to the stage than to the audience, they are certainly a body of people in a high state of interested excitement; and if they are to add the interest of the play itself instead of detracting from it, the Chorus on the modern stage must be represented by people who utter their comments, whether they be reflections or passionate expressions of pity or rejoicing, like people naturally moved. In their treatment of the Greek Chorus, Messrs. Vedrenne and Barker seem to have lapsed for the first and only time from their guiding principle of production. A chorus of men would probably be more effective; for the voices of men speaking together are much more impressive, and they look and move far better than women in the Greek dress, who for some reason or other appear self-conscious.

Before considering the performances in detail it will be well to review at a glance the work of these two and a half years.*

---

*For dates and the number of performances given of each play, see Appendix I.

Shaw . . . . . eleven plays .	*Candida.*	
	John Bull's Other Island.	
	How he Lied to Her Husband.	
	You Never Can Tell.	
	Man and Superman.	
	Major Barbara.	
	Captain Brassbound's Conversion.	
	The Doctor's Dilemma.	
	The Philanderer.	
	Don Juan in Hell.	
	The Man of Destiny.	
Euripides . . . . three plays .	*Hippolytus.*	
	The Trojan Women.	
	Electra.	
Ibsen . . . . two plays .	*The Wild Duck.*	
	Hedda Gabler.	
Hankin . . . . . . two plays .	*The Return of the Prodigal.*	
	The Charity that Began at Home.	
Hewlett . . . . . . two plays .	*Pan and the Young Shepherd.*	
	The Youngest of the Angels.	
Barker	*The Voysey Inheritance.*	
Housman, Barker, and Moorat . .	*Prunella.*	
Galsworthy	*The Silver Box.*	
Hauptman	*The Thieves' Comedy.*	
Elizabeth Robins	*Votes for Women !*	
Schnitzler	*In the Hospital.*	
Robert Vernon Harcourt	*A Question of Age.*	
Cyril Harcourt	*The Reformer.*	
Masefield	*The Campden Wonder.*	
Maeterlinck	*Aglavaine and Selysette.*	
Fenn	*The Convict on the Hearth.*	
Yeats	*The Pot of Broth.*	

No one can help being struck by the number and variety of these plays; no other modern managers have given so many memorable performances in so short a space of time.

CHAPTER II

The Court Theatre Dramatists

THE young dramatists, whose plays have been performed at the Court, differ from each other in so many respects that they cannot be readily classified. There is, however, one broad distinction which can be made between some and others. The work of Mr. Granville Barker, Mr. Galsworthy and, in a lesser degree, of Mr. Hankin shows a critical, dissenting attitude towards contemporary codes of morality; while, on the other hand, Mr. Robert Vernon Harcourt and Mr. Cyril Harcourt and Mr. Fenn take the world as a going concern. Mr. Granville Barker's treatment of a case of conscience in *The Voysey Inheritance* is distinctly subversive. The moral is that embezzlement with the view of straightening out a crooked state of things may be the right course for a young man who finds himself heir to a business founded on fraud; in fact, the whole play is directed against the notion that questions of right and wrong can be decided by rules of thumb. Mr. Galsworthy's play *The Silver Box* is an attack on the injustice of our present social machinery. The play presents two instances of exactly similar offences, the one committed by the idle good-for-nothing son of a rich man, the other by a surly, unpleasant, but by no means despicable workman, and shows how the former escapes and the latter is punished. The great merit of this play is the complex exactness of the parallel between the two cases, which nevertheless is so unobtrusively drawn that the fact that there is a moral only occurs to the spectator during the last act; this is the highest compliment which can be paid to a play with a purpose, that the moral is not perceived till the end.

In the case of Mr. Hankin it is more difficult to show that there is anything of the reformer about him; but certainly the distribution of sympathy in *The Return of the Prodigal* is not conventional. In that play he puts forward a good case for a real ne'er-do-well, who has about him no touch of the stage romance which usually surrounds such a character.

On the other hand the man who has the *beau role* in Mr. Fenn's *Convict on the Hearth*, is an East End parson who makes everybody happy by the most approved methods of cheerful Christian sympathy. It is an amusing, friendly, touching little piece; but with no more criticism of current ideas in it than there is in *The Christmas Carol*. Both Mr. Harcourts take the world of fashion as they find it, and they find it—simply very amusing.

In spite, then, of the preponderance of Mr. Shaw and the presence of Ibsen in the play-bills, it cannot be said that the Court Theatre represented only one movement of thought, even were the classical plays and such romantic plays as *Pan and the Young Shepherd, Aglavaine and Selysette,* and *Prunella* are set on one side. But it has represented an æsthetic and dramatic movement of remarkably wide sympathies. Messrs. Vedrenne and Barker have produced a number of plays which have been attacks on current ideas, and they have produced others in which the morality is of the customary type; they have produced plays so unconventional in form and construction that no other manager in London would look at them, and plays such as *The Reformer,* by Mr. Cyril Harcourt, which in method and tone resembles the ordinary society play. Whatever was good of its kind was given its chance, but the number of the plays without what is considered a good construction among them is a significant fact. If the æsthetic influence of the Court Theatre upon the modern drama were capable of being summed up in a sentence, the truest summary would be that it has expanded enormously the conception of what kind of story is suitable for the stage; in short, that it has enlarged the meaning of the word "dramatic," for that adjective signifies nothing but a quality in actions and persons which would make them impressive on the stage. It used to be held, and is still very generally believed, that the plot was the most important part of the play. The playwright constructed his plot and then made the characters as real as he could within the limits it allowed. He proceeded along certain recognized lines. The first act, and sometimes the second act as well, was employed in drawing the characters and indicating their surroundings in such a way that there was no need to return to them again; the intrigue or plot probably began in the second act, and grew more and more complicated until it was quickly unravelled in the third or fourth according to the length of the play. Whether the play was a good one or not depended chiefly upon the intensity with which the audience was made to wonder how on earth the characters were going to get out of their particular fix, how the compromising letter would be recovered, or the misunderstanding cleared up. Ingenuity of construction was, then, an absolutely essential quality in a dramatist. If he could draw character as well, or create situations of emotional interest, he was a good dramatist; but neither of these powers by themselves served to win him that reputation or even to get his plays acted at all. The exposition in the first act was often immensely more interesting than either the plot or the *denouement,* but the play was condemned if these were not neatly contrived. The result of this tradition was to prevent a number of writers, who had greater power of communicating emotion and a far greater understanding of human nature than many successful playwrights, from writing for the stage at all. Either they did not possess the degree of ingenuity necessary to construct a plot, or they were bored with having to treat the problems arising out of character and circumstance mechanically.

The tendency of modern dramatic art is now to make the characters and the emotional and moral significance of the situations the most important elements, and to reduce the plot to a minimum. The characters in consequence are not merely presented during the early scenes, but go on developing till the end of the play, so that the spectator may have to alter his first impressions. In consequence, the faculty upon which the modern play tends to rely more and more in the spectator is no longer the power of following the indications of a complex story, but of seizing and remembering shades of character and emotion; and the spectator's pleasure depends now not so much on being unable to guess what is going to happen next, as in being able to recognize that what does happen next is true and interesting, either as a fact in human nature or as proving or disproving some theory or belief. Of course good construction is necessary in every play. The stage always makes the most rigid economy of incidents necessary, and if one event can be made to serve the purposes of illustrating several points, so much the better; but the revolt against "the well-constructed" play is, on one side, a denial of the statement that every play in order to be good must have the same kind of construction, and, on the other, the assertion that character and nature are more interesting on the stage (as elsewhere) than a cunningly dovetailed series of unlikely events, and that they are therefore in reality more "dramatic." This does not, of course, imply that all situations and developments of character are "dramatic" simply because they are interesting; nor does it get rid of the necessity for "action" in a play, for "action" is the quickest and most vivid way of exhibiting character. But it must be remembered that action may be internal as well as external. It is, then, a protest against the condemnation of a play which has succeeded in being interesting, on the ground that there is not enough "action" in it, or because it does not keep the audience in doubt about the manner in which it will end.

If the emotions and relations between the characters in any story or situation are of the kind which admit of being represented interestingly in the limited time the theatre allows, then, as long as a dramatist succeeds in this, it is absurd to find fault with him; but if they can only be interesting or beautiful when their gradual, minute, internal development is shown, then they are not the subject-matter for the dramatist, but for the novelist. The danger besetting the new school is in the choice of subjects simply on account of their interest from the point of view of either psychology or morals, without paying enough regard to this distinction; the justification of their principles is that their works have increased enormously the importance and interest of the theatre.

The first characteristic of Mr. Hankin as a dramatist is that he is easy to act; his characters are very clearly drawn, and the emotions and situations with which his plays deal are within the reach of a very moderate range of experience. The parts do not call for "temperament" or imagination in the actors so much as intelligence and sympathy, which are easier to find. His other qualities are lightness of touch, an original humour, the power of weighing character in a very even balance, and dexterity in introducing into a very ordinary series of events, which the audience is certain will be evolved along the most natural lines, an element of surprise and suspense. *The Return of the Prodigal* shows all these qualities at their best.

The party at the Jacksons' house has just broken up, when the butler rushes in to say that the Master Eustace, whom all believed to be in Australia, is lying lifeless on the doorstep. There is a moment of wild excitement and agitation, and a pale, mud-bespattered youth is carried in and laid upon the sofa. Will he revive? Certainly some instinctive tenderness for him revives in the bosom of his family. In the frantic search for restoratives he is left alone for a moment, when the audience is surprised to see him coolly raise himself and settle again more comfortably into a dead faint. Amid cries of "My darling boy!" "He's not dead!" "He's coming to!" the curtain falls. One is very curious to know what sort of a scapegrace he will turn out to be. He turns out a limp, cleverish fellow with a firm conviction of his own utter incompetence. He has knocked about the world, lost the money he was sent out with, and now, tired and mildly reckless, he has come home to enjoy again the comforts of clean clothes, rest, and a little indulgence, even if he has to pose as a wreck to get them. What is to become of him? What on earth are his family to do with him? That is the interest of the play, and it is sustained to the end. His mother and sister are glad enough to pet him; but after he has loafed about the house some days, and even the country doctor can no longer pretend that there is anything the matter with him, his brother and his father come down with the question, "What do you propose to do?" He answers: "Nothing. I can't do anything. What do *you* propose to do?" He has told his brother in confidence that his physical collapse on the night of his arrival was a bit of acting to rouse sympathy, thus making him an irritated accomplice in his success. Both father and brother are fretting to get rid of him. He regards them as a couple of heartless humbugs, who exploit others, and, being slaves to snobbish aims, can for once be exploited by himself. When a tailor's bill comes in, and his father in a fit of desperation threatens to turn him out of the house, the Prodigal simply replies: "Very well. I shall go to the nearest workhouse, and do you think you will get into Parliament if the constituency hears that you, a wealthy manufacturer, have driven your son to the workhouse?" To his brother he says: "Do you suppose you will succeed in uniting yourself to a good county family (especially as the girl doesn't care for you, and even likes me better) if there is such a horrid scandal in your own?" He has them in a cleft stick. In the last act they propose to send him off to Australia again with another £1,000. He refuses that, for he would simply lose it as he did the first thousand and starve again. He holds out for £250 a year, and promises never to show his face in future without request. He takes a cheque for his first quarter's allowance, and departs that very night to avoid seeing his fond, foolish old mother again.

This may seem a slender theme for a play, and the solution of a problem, into which the spectator has entered with an almost parental perplexity, by the allowance of £250 may sound flat; but the *dénouement* is not flat, and the suspense is kept up till the last. The dialogue is most spirited and natural, and often extremely amusing. The Prodigal excites a good deal of sympathy, because he is moved by the sympathy of his mother and sister, and because he is miserable and aware of his own feebleness, which he makes the justification of his claim, as he really believes himself incapable of earning a living; while a scene between brother and sister, very touching in its matter-of-factness, makes one feel that father and son are fair game, by revealing that her prospects of a free and happy future have been ruined by being dragged by them into a society where for her there is little chance of marriage. Stella Faringford will probably marry Henry Jackson. Some kind of a love-liking springs up between her and the Prodigal in the course of the four acts, just enough to make the sense of his own incompetence harder to bear and the conclusion of the play doubtful.

The Charity that Began at Home is not so good. At the close of the play you are left in doubt as to which characters are meant to be in the right and which in the wrong; and this is here a defect, because they are divided into two groups holding opposite views of life. Lady Denison and Margery and Hylton make living for others their rule of life, and act on the assumption that every one is good at bottom, and that only kindness is required to make them behave well; while Hugh Verreker and Mrs. Eversleigh take the view of human nature upon which the ordinary judgments of the law and society rest.

Lady Denison is a delightful character, and she was delightfully played by Miss Florence Haydon. Her art is based upon a kindly, humorous, and minute observation, in quality something akin to Mr. Haskin's own comic perception, namely a subtle relish for inconsequence of speech, and for a kind of unconscious wit, which results from an intelligent muddleheadedness. This cosy, acquiescing, scatter-brained old lady obeys the promptings of a soft heart, with many sighs over the quandaries in which it lands her, only less bewildering and painful to her than would be the alternative of showing severity. Her remark while protesting against Hylton's argument that the butler, in spite of having seduced the maid, must be allowed to stop on, reveals her. "I may save a soul," says Hylton. "Oh, how very annoying!" she exclaims, and decides at once to keep him. On the other hand, when she learns that her daughter is engaged to Verreker, whose shady past has just been revealed, she is very much upset and shocked, notwithstanding her "belief" in everybody's underlying goodness. Mrs. Eversleigh, after saying "This comes of your idiotic principle of being kind to worthless people," asks her, with asperity, what step she proposes to take. "I shall dismiss Soames," she answers firmly, pressing the electric bell (Act II curtain). Truly a very inconsequent old lady! But she is very real and convincing.

The Silver Box was most admirably performed. It is **Mr.** Galsworthy's triumph to have contrived to be subtle without intricacy, and the triumph of the actors and management to have represented the scenes with so much nature and minute accuracy. Very seldom has a performance so careful had at the same time so much the air of a play that acted itself. Mr. Galsworthy's qualities as a dramatist are precision of design, a well-poised estimate of human nature, and the command of cool well-considered satire, which is the more effective for being unexcited, and the more remarkable for being combined with a strong interest in social questions.

The first act takes place in the dining-room of John Barthwick's heavy rich house. His son Jack (perfectly played by Mr. A. E. Matthews) returns drunk between twelve and one at night. He has got in with the help of a workman who happened to see him fumbling at the keyhole. Jack enters, in a state of sordid exhilaration, waving a reticule which he has snatched away "for a rag" from the woman in whose flat he has spent the evening. He offers Jones the workman, who has sulkily followed him in, a drink, as he has not got a tip in his pocket. Jones, who has been looking for work all day on an empty stomach, takes a stiff glass of whisky, with the result that it flies to his head. He is not at all a bad sort of man; but he is down on his luck and gloomily resentful against a world which treats him badly. Mr. McKinnel conveyed his character perfectly. After apostrophizing the torpid Jack, he snatches up the woman's purse and the Barthwicks' silver cigarette-box and goes out. The impulse which makes him take them is exactly the same kind of drunken spite which made Jack carry off the reticule from its owner. Next morning, when the box is missed, suspicion falls on Mrs. Jones, who is the Barthwicks' charwoman, and in the next act her room is searched and she is arrested as well as her husband, who loudly protests that he alone is guilty. The Unknown Lady has meanwhile called to recover her purse; Jack's escapade is revealed, and his father, who refunds the missing money, naturally wishes to hush up the whole matter. But the prosecution cannot now be withdrawn, and the last act is laid in a London police-court. The charge against the Joneses is the theft of the box. By the help of the Barthwicks' solicitor, who takes advantage of Jack's cowardice and muddled recollection of the night's doings, the magistrate is persuaded that Jones got into the house through Jack having left his key in the door; this task is facilitated by Jones' truculent clamours for justice. Mrs. Jones is discharged; Jones gets a month's hard labour; and Jack leaves the court as a young scapegrace who has deserved indulgent reproof.

One of Mr. R. V. Harcourt's merits as a playwriter is his dialogue, which reflects better, I think, than that of any other dramatist's, the offhand sparkle and exhilaration of the lives of the children of leisure and pleasure. Mr. Sutro makes such people wickedly epigrammatic and very vulgar; Mr. Arthur Jones can hardly be said to be successful in such characters; Mr. Pinero reproduces this atmosphere well, but still he does not get it quite right. It is a society in which the fools are apt to show quick intelligence and "the gifted what seems to the thoughtful an extraordinary limitation of view." The peculiar quality does not lie only in a frank avowal of having an eye to the main chance and of the permanency of natural instincts. Mr. Pinero seems to me to miss in his plays a kind flexibility of feeling in these people, which, I think, Mr. Harcourt is very happy in rendering. This gift of writing society dialogue will stand him in good stead, and there is little doubt that to it he chiefly owes the acceptance of the plays he has already written.

But the chief merit in Mr. Harcourt's plays, the merit which induces me to back him for success, is the cause also of his present failure. His best quality is his acute and intricate sense of a situation. His sense of it is so complete that he cannot bear to prune it down to bare issues; and so, not having any particular deftness in stage craft, he naturally involves himself and his audience in perplexity.

His play *A Question of Age* missed fire for this reason. The story is one of cross-purposes. A widow on the verge of middle age tries to persuade a young man to become her lover, who is trying to screw up his mind to marry her for her money, and the complication arises out of each misunderstanding what the other wants.

Partly owing to an unfortunate omission in the dialogue at the first performance, the situation was still further embroiled. Miss Fanny Brough and Mr. Kerr were both excellent in their parts.

The most remarkable feature of *The Voysey Inheritance* is the skill with which the interest in a single situation is maintained through four acts; that this is a sign of fertility and not poverty of imagination all who have ever tried to write know well. Its second great merit is the vividness with which a large family is presented, each member of which is a distinct character. The second act is like a good chapter from a novel read at a happy moment of hallucination.

The men are sitting round the decanters and dessert. Major Booth Voysey (admirably played by Mr. Charles Fulton) is straddling in front of the fire and laying down the law in a loud, hectoring voice; his father bends over his plate, cracking nuts and occasionally directing an acid remark at him. Old Mr. Booth and the vicar are at the table, unconscious victims of their host's financial talents; an engaged daughter skips in and, glorying archly in the emancipation of her position, carries off her rather shame-faced betrothed to the solitude of the billiard-room; Honor, "Mother's right hand," a nervous, slavishly unselfish, quite helpless old maid, bustles in and out in a distressed way on her brother's errands.

Mr. Voysey, the father of the family, has speculated all his life with the sums entrusted to his care as a solicitor; at first to make up for the defalcations of his father, but afterwards, so it turns out, because he could not resist the temptation to use his financial talent. At the opening of the play he is in arrears again, owing to some unfortunate speculations; and on admitting his son Edward into the partnership he reveals the trick to him. It is, he says, "The Voysey Inheritance," and he adds that strangely enough it has been the cause of his happiness, for after years of keeping his courage to the sticking place he enjoys a perpetual exhilaration from feeling under his feet the thinness of the crust on which his prosperous home is built. He is an admirable study. Edward is at first deeply shocked and troubled; but when his father dies suddenly he takes up the Voysey inheritance and continues to speculate with the client's money in order to refund those who would feel the loss most. By taking this decision he wins the regard of a girl he had long wanted to marry, and in her mouth is put the moral of the piece. She exhorts him to be a man and to go through with it, for he is only risking the money of the rich to pay back the poor. He does not, however, inspire the same confidence as his father, and when old Mr. Booth comes to the office to demand back his securities, Edward tells him everything. He is too sick of the whole business to care much what happens. Booth threatens to prosecute if he is not paid back at the rate of £1,000 a year, a condition which would prevent Edward refunding the money of men who have far less than old Booth. He refuses—and the matter is dropped. The fact that the play stops at this point is a defect, and it is a defect very characteristic of this school of dramatists. The interest of the author has been centred entirely on the moral development of the hero, and the growth in him of a new way of looking at life, with the consequence that when this has been accomplished subsequent developments do not appear to the dramatist important. Still, the audience would like to know whether old Booth did prosecute or not; and the fact that the curtain falls at a juncture which rouses curiosity instead of satisfying it is a defect.

Prunella is a real Pierrot play. In what region of Europe an inventive mind brought forth the creature *Pierrot*, or among what popular imaginations he was first kindly fostered and formed, I do not know; whether, like Punchinello and Columbina, he crossed the Alps of Italy, or whether he bears by birthright his French name. But this may be taken as certain, that he was born in the Latin zone, beyond the influence of Northern tenderness and Northern seriousness. For, though the peculiar blend of human sentiment which he engenders and embodies contains both seriousness and tenderness, they are of a kind so inimical to ours, that we instinctively condemn them as hardness and frivolity. If there are virtues which Pierrot hates, they are dignity, self-respect, and consistency. He has never been able to take life more seriously, as far as behaviour is concerned, than his own amusing mummeries, and men have found him pleasant company because he is so shockingly free from any sense of responsibility. He flatters their self-importance by his contrasted flimsiness, and the gravid mind enjoys vicariously in him a light-heeled dance. Yet he is not gay. He would lose many of his boon companions if he were; since true gaiety does not flatter in itself; rather it dismays those who cannot accompany its towerings. It cannot be patronized; Pierrot can be. He often whimpers for a little pity, hiding his need in comic antics, in case he should not be understood. True, if you give it him, when he thinks he has not betrayed the craving, you may be startled by a flare of pride; but it is a flash in a shallow pan, and if you pity him again he will melt. If you could get him to philosophize quietly upon himself, without crowing like a cock or pouring the wine on your head, you would probably find that the one virtue upon which he prided himself was humility. He would say that nobody in the world seemed humble except himself; if you said, "That sounds rather like a contradiction in terms," he would not be the least disconcerted. He might go on to confide that the want of humility in everybody else seemed to him, when he was in good spirits, the most grotesquely funny thing in the world, but that oftener it simply crushed him. No one, he would add, who cultivated a sense of responsibility could have humility; such a sense was in itself a proof of arrogance. He feels his humility will take him to heaven.

All this may seem to have very little to do with the play; but it does concern the *sentiment* of the play. For this is a real Pierrot play; not a fake. It may be careless here and there; but it is not a fake. Therefore, the sentiment of Pierrot must be understood, if the play is to be appreciated, and, above all, this "humility," which is so unsympathetic to the majority of us, who, whatever opinions we may have about art or the body or pleasure, have an ascetic repugnance to any intimate form of self-abandonment, feeling that humility is less than reverence, and that reverence implies a restraint of emotion, whether in religion, love, or sympathy. So much for Pierrot. I can only give an idea of the play by trying to describe one or two scenes; to tell the story baldly would destroy the sentiment.

In a correct and charming garden, situated it does not matter where, one summer's morning, it does not matter when, for this is the kingdom of fancy, are sitting three prim maiden ladies, outside their staid old red-brick house. Near to a high yew hedge stands a dry fountain over which a figure representing Love presides, his chin upon a fiddle. A little girl, say sixteen years old, sits some few paces off them, reading out her lesson in a monotonous sing-song. Prunella reads and reads, and the ladies, her severe, particular aunts, begin to yawn and then to nod and then to sleep. And as she reads she is aware of a merry, bewildering music; faint at first, then nearer and nearer; she holds her breath; she gabbles faster and faster; louder and louder it sounds; it draws her like an eddy; the maiden aunts wake with a horrified jump and bustle into the house; over the high, thick hedge come paper startlers and handfuls of confetti; the din grows chaotic and rowdy—whistles and catcalls and songs—as the mystic mummers go by on the road of the outside world. Prunella, panting with excitement, stands tiptoe on a chair to peep over. Then, at her feet she sees Pierrot crouching; head adroop in whimsical adoration, geranium lips pouted to an O, black eyebrows arched in a blank white stare. "What are you doing here, you beautiful white boy?" Presently, the whole band are round her, dancing and laughing and tempting and teasing —Scaramel, Kennel and Callow, Tawdry and Doll and Romp; and Prunella at last gives Pierrot a kiss, to ease him of his elaborate pain.

Another scene: it is moonlight, and the house is shut. Pierrot, seated in pensive expectation on the rim of the fountain, is serenading her window, vicariously, through the voice of Tenor, dressed like him. The mandolin tinkles and quavers; the stars seem to throb. The song stops; and Pierrot advances underneath her window. All is silent; Scaramel fetches a ladder: "Little bird in your nest, are you there?" Slowly the window opens, and Prunella, her hair flying a tattery dark cloud upon her shoulders, kneels in the window. Quietly the garden begins to fill with fantastic figures; they dance and beckon, mopping and mowing, whispering and laughing. Pierrot calls to her to come down. Then follows a love duet, the dissonant harmony of which I shall not try to suggest. They strew flowers before her and crown her bewildered head, and call her Pierrette. Before she yields, she kneels before the statute of Love, imploring his oracle. The figure begins to live, the bow to slowly move across the strings, and the marble instrument to sound, "drawing out her soul like a spider's thread." The statue bids her go with her lover.

Some years have past. It is autumn; the dry leaves scuttle drearily down the weedy garden paths. Two of the sisters are dead, and Privacy, the last of them, has lived on alone, hoping Prunella would come back. She is poor, and the house has been bought by a mysterious rich gentleman. This day he is to take possession. He enters, dressed in black; it is Lord Pierrot. He first deserted, and then he lost Pierrette. He has come to live in "The Dutch Garden," that he may, if possible, lay the ghost of his love. To-night he has called his old companions round him to dispel his miserable regrets. They are withered and spiritless now, and it is but a death's-head feast they can hold together. Pierrette, a wandering beggar-girl, comes back, too, while they are eating and drinking inside the house; and after reproaching Love for his deception, she falls asleep in the fountain basin. Pierrot, in an agony of self-reproach, acts over again the window-scene of his wooing of Prunella and once more kneels at the fountain. . . . For the last time the statue speaks, and all is happy.

The actors seemed to enjoy their parts. They certainly played most admirably. Miss Dorothy Minton was enrapturing as Prunella, and Mr. Graham Browne's Pierrot was a work of art. The music followed and expressed every turn of the sentiment.

Before going on to the plays by foreign dramatists a word must be said about Mr. Masefield's short play, *The Campden*

Wonder. It is a story taken from the history of Campden, where in 1666 two men and their old mother were hung on the confession, steadily adhered to, of one of the sons, that they had murdered a man who afterward turned out to be alive. The motive of this murderous bit of perjury has never been discovered. Mr. Masefield has invented a motive. The elder, a drunken sot, is determined to degrade his mild, steady brother. In the first scene the brothers quarrel; this scene is admirable: in the second he confesses before a muddle-headed old parson: in the third all three are in gaol, and one by one they are taken out and hanged. The wife of the supposed victim arrives too late with the news that she has seen her husband. The old woman whimpers distressingly, the young brother howls and pleads for his life, and cries out for his wife and children, the elder (admirably played by Mr. Norman McKinnel) hugs himself with a kind of insane, sardonic rapture at his triumph. He has stuck to his lie with a dogged, hulking stupidity—"For un's gowld un did it." His psychology, the presentation of a mind in which malignity is mixed with the stupidity of madness, is the author's best success. The dialogue of some of the scenes is written with a force and directness which has a marked æsthetic quality; but the performance was not satisfactory.

This piece, again, is most characteristic, in its merits and its weakness, of the new school. Where is the plot? What is the point? were the questions asked. The answer is that it does not pretend to have either plot or moral; it is simply a tragic story and a piece of life—"and life, some think, is worthy of the Muse."

[For the following account of a play which I missed I am indebted to a friend.]

Votes for Women! by Miss Elizabeth Robins, was called "a dramatic tract." The story of the play, which was almost entirely confined to the first and third acts, was dramatic indeed—even melodramatic; but, as far as the propaganda of the Woman Suffrage party is concerned, it probably disappointed the most ardent supporters of the movement, who would anticipate, from the use of the word "tract," that the play would champion the demand for the extension of the franchise. It did indeed do so, but indirectly, by including that demands for "votes" in the more important demand for "rights." Put shortly, the problem lay in the relations of the three principal characters—relations by no means new to the stage. Geoffrey Stonor, a man of rank and position in social and parliamentary circles, affianced to Beatrice Dunbarton, a young lady of his own standing, meets by accident Vida Levering, with whom he had lived in earlier days. The last act of the play is devoted to the re-adjustment of the relative positions of these three characters, in the light of a complete understanding on the part of each.

Written throughout with the customary cleverness of the author, the play was chiefly remarkable for a brilliant piece of realism in the second act. Author, stage-manager, and actors combined to give a vivid representation of a suffragist meeting in Trafalgar Square, which was applauded alike by those who went to see a play and those who went to hear their cause promoted. The working woman, the youthful enthusiast, and the male champion (one of Mr. Edmund Gwenn's greatest triumphs) were all represented, and Vida Levering (admirably played by Miss Wynne-Matthison) spoke from her own sad experience. Most successful of all, however, was the crowd on the stage, comprising every type of a Trafalgar Square audience, and overflowing with the usual impromptu comments—earnest, sarcastic, approving, flippant, intoxicated. In short, this stage-audience represented the Chorus in a Greek play more nearly than anything in English drama since *The Knight of the Burning Pestle*, in as much as they gave vent to the gnomic and critical remarks of the ordinary spectator.

FOREIGN PLAYS

Aglavaine and Selysette was not impressive, though sometimes it was really moving. It is the story of a child-wife whose husband meets a woman he can love more seriously. Aglavaine and he both have a tender love for "little Selysette";

but they know their feelings for each other are the best they have ever felt, and they hope that Selysette will go on being happy in the kind of love her husband has always given her, nor be pained by the sight of an intimacy her nature cannot understand. But Selysette does understand one thing—that she is in the way; and so she jumps down from a tower and is killed. Now it is absolutely necessary, in order to feel what the author intends, that we should believe the man and the woman to be very wonderful people; and the fault of the play is that we have to take this for granted instead of being made to believe it. Both of them do nothing but talk of their love, and kiss and pity "little Selysette." Mr. Donald Tovey's music was beautiful.

Herr Schnitzler's play *In the Hospital* is a pure bit of psychology. Karl Rademacher, an author, is dying in the General Hospital. His last request is that a friend of his youth, now a successful literary quack, should visit him. He wants to revenge his failure by proving that he was the lover of this man's wife, and that she knew him for the better man. He works himself into such a frenzy of vindictive delight at the thought of the blow he is going to strike at this sleek humbug, that he almost dies. Mr. Beveridge acted with both intensity and restraint. The literary man comes to his side after the paroxysm, and Rademacher dies without telling him a word, for when he sees him it does not seem worth while, and then he has already slaked in imagination his thirst for revenge.

The performance of *The Wild Duck* at the Court Theatre was rather disappointing. Though each part was admirably played, as a whole it was not so impressive as the performance of Herr Andresen's company at the German Theatre last winter. This was due firstly to the actors taking some scenes too fast, and secondly to the peculiarity of Mr. Granville Barker's rendering of Hialmar, though in itself it was an accomplished and consistent piece of acting.

His Hialmar Ekdal was a pitiable and ridiculous figure, instead of a repulsive and ridiculous one; for though many may deny the harsh impeachment, Hialmar is a wide shot that hits half the world. But that he should be represented as disgusting, repulsive, revolting, as well as ridiculous, is absolutely essential if the unity of the play is to be maintained. If any scene in *The Wild Duck* is played as simple comedy, if your laughter is not always on the wrong side of your mouth, the meaning of the play is obscured, and the suicide of Hedvig at the end will seem the wilful work of a morbid pessimist who sets down things in malice.

Ibsen's work seems that of a man who started life self-distrusting, modest, and ready to admire, and found out at last that men whom he thought better were in reality worse than himself. There is a kind of hard pity in this play which speaks most distinctly in the mouth of Relling, who has kept alive that modicum of self-respect necessary to life in the poor wrecks of humanity he meets, by fostering in them what he calls their "life illusions." Ibsen allows no good nature in art, and the fault we have to find with Mr. Barker's interpretation is that it is too good-natured. He played Hialmar as though he were a creation of the relenting and vivacious satire of Mr. Shaw, who is always careful to let every character state his case, to lend him the brains of a devil's advocate for the occasion, and not only to show the very pulse of the machine but to lecture to the audience upon its working. Though it would be absurd to say that Mr. Barker intentionally took the audience into his confidence, he often emphasized too consciously the ironic intentions of the dramatist. If Hedvig at the end had emerged from the sliding doors of the garret and made an irrefutable little speech, asserting her intention to get a comfortable settlement out of Werle, and explaining that her father did not really care two straws whose child she was, it would not have been very incongruous with the spirit in which some of the scenes were played. No, that is saying too much; but if this statement is taken with a large pinch of salt, readers of the play will get an idea of what was disappointing in the performance of many fine bits of acting.

Mr. George, as old Ekdal, was good, specially in the first act, when Hialmar, Gregers (the idealist), and he are drinking their beer together. His tipsy winks and dark hints that his hunting days are not over, his determination that very night to show the garret, with its strange contents, withered Christmas trees, sleeping fowls and rabbits, and the cherished *wild duck* snug in her basket, all these were admirable. The group round the garret door, the mysterious moonlit peep within, the old man with upraised lamp, his proud chuckling replies to the guests' astonished questions, Hialmar's simulated indifference, and the child's eager explanations made up a scene not easy to forget; while in the foreground sat the anxious, silent woman, who keeps these creatures fed and housed, hugging her shawl about her with a shiver, feeling, not understanding, the shame and shirking which such substitutes for real life mean.

Miss Agnes Thomas was the best English Gina I remember. The only criticism which can be made upon her interpretation, which was complete in itself, is that it is not the most interesting one possible. She emphasized the impatience which can be read into Gina's replies; but these are most impressive when they are spoken passively in self-defense. The Gina most worth acting is the Gina who, padding about in her felt slippers, never doubts for a moment that she should do everything for those she loves, and, unless she is defending her husband from criticism, which she is quick to scent far off, dimly feels what Relling the philosopher understands; and to act her thus the superficial comedy of her clumsy simplicity must never quite distract attention from the delicacy of her nature, which finds expression in that moving exclamation when Hedvig lies dead, while Hialmar rants over her, and Relling looks down at her with professional detachment, "The child mustn't lie here for a show."

One moment Miss Thomas succeeded in stamping on the imagination with a force no actress could have bettered; the moment when she rounds on Hialmar's petulant, bullying questions about Hedvig's parentage with "I don't know — how can I tell—a creature like me?" In her voice and gesture you feel indignation, revolt, and shame. This was Hialmar's best scene, too, unless he was as admirable when he repulsed

Hedvig, with hysterical gesticulations of abhorrence, and dashed like a maniac from the house. Miss Dorothy Minto's Hedvig was particularly good. But she missed expressing to the full the blank dismay of horror Hedvig must have felt, when her sulky father, looking into the sitting-room the morning after his debauch, tells her to get out, and holds the door open, glowering soddenly at her, without a word. It is the last time she sees her father, and she cannot understand. That walk across the stage to the kitchen is an important incident, if we are to be convinced that Hedvig would have shot herself.

Mr. Lang's Relling could have only been improved in one respect, which was not in his power to remedy. In casting the part of Relling, I believe the important quality to look for in the personality of the actor is his voice. As this may seem a fanciful flight of criticism, it is necessary to explain; for it rests on a conception of the character which may not be shared. Relling has been described by Brandes as a humorous personification of Ibsen himself, and certainly the moral of the piece speaks through his mouth; but this definition of him is far from the truth. He, too, has gone to seed, though he remains a sort of doctor still, and still can help the spiritually sick by hiding their natures from their own eyes; that is his universal remedy. But the secret of his peculiar blend of bitter tenderness and cynical leniency lies in his own character. If you met him you would see in his eyes that he had defrauded his own soul. Now, you cannot get an impression from a person on the stage in that subtle way; but you can hear it in a voice. The actor, then, to play Relling is a man whose voice contrasts oddly, disagreeably, though sometimes the sound of it brings a sense of relief, with the grating things he says. This is a personal impression, of course, and must be taken for what it is worth. You should hear something like despair in his voice, however trenchant and contemptuous his manner of speaking when he pronounces his famous dictum, "Life would be quite tolerable if only we could get rid of the confounded duns that keep on pestering us in our poverty with the claims of the ideal."

Many think *The Wild Duck* the best of Ibsen's prose dramas. There is certainly none which shows a completer mastery of stage craft. It must have astonished his admirers when it first appeared; for it looks like a satire on his own philosophy. It is an assault on "Ibsenites," on men and women who think that to blurt out the truth and destroy everything which has an alloy of compromise and sham in it, is the sure remedy for social and private evils. Nothing Ibsen has written makes us respect him more. He had always declared that, "What is wanted is a revolution in the spirit of man"; in this play he faces the reformer's worst trial, the conviction of the fundamental weakness of human nature.

The performance of *Hedda Gabler* was better than that of *The Wild Duck*. It is seldom so remarkable a play is so remarkably acted. Mrs. Patrick Campbell's acting of Hedda was not one hair's-breadth out. Hedda, as a character, strikes us as at once monstrous and familiar. She is a woman who considers herself *déplacée*, not merely by having married out of a fast, fashionable set, and taken a humdrum bookish man, with irritating little habits, for a husband; but one who considers herself *déplacée* in the world itself. She is bored to death, like Madame Bovary—the marvel is that the psychology of Flaubert's novel is compressed into this astonishing play— but, unlike Emma Bovary, having experienced the delights of the children of leisure and pleasure she cherishes no illusions about them. "She has danced till she was tired." The whole of life appears to her mean and wretched, child-bearing a particularly odious humiliation, love a fraud, and even an illicit intrigue too "banal" to have any attraction. She prides herself on her boredom, lassitude and disgust, taking them for signs of an aristocratic spirit, which the experiences of vulgar souls can never satisfy. Living in a permanent condition of sulky conceit, her only pleasure lies in swaggering; and since her circumstances are too narrow for display, she falls back on inflicting petty humiliations on those in her power, like her aunt Nora. It follows from this sullen arrogance that the one thing she cannot bear the thought of is—humiliation; hence her dread of scandal, of being mixed up in anything shameful and sordid, like Lövborg's death; hence the power of Judge Brack's threat to involve her in it; hence her preference for suicide to remaining at his mercy; hence, too, the explanation of her never having yielded to an attraction for Lövborg or for any other man. Her ruling passion prevents her ever giving herself away. She could only marry a man she despised. This stupid, sullen conceit is like a wall dividing her from life; she cannot throw herself into anything without dispelling her cherished illusion of superiority; she is only safe in acting upon others from a superior height. She is envious and loves power; she therefore drags Lövborg down out of a kind of cold malignity, warmed by a little jealousy of Mrs. Elvsted, much as Iago's dispassionate hatred is just touched by a little lust for Desdemona. Like Iago, she is a kind of inarticulate playwright, too stupid to imagine, who gratifies at once a longing for power and a love of excitement by using human beings as puppets. This is the source of Hedda's impulse to make Lövborg drink, that she may see him "with vine-leaves in his hair," and to shoot himself, that she may know that "beautiful actions" are possible.

Mrs. Patrick Campbell became this character to the life. It speaks wonders for the Court Theatre management that she did not act the others off the stage.

Mr. Trevor Lowe, as George Tesman, Hedda's husband, was excellent, and Mr. James Hearn's Judge Brack was a good piece of careful acting. Lövborg's entrance the morning after the debauch, in which he has lost his manuscript and his self-respect, was most impressive. Mr. Laurence Irving can, as the phrase is, "look volumes." It is a rare power; and this faculty, of standing silently and suggesting in attitude and face an intense state of emotion, is perhaps the most remarkable of his talents.

Two defects came out in the play; one of them is an unlikely bit of human nature, the other is a defect which the inevitable compression of the dramatic form forces on Ibsen. The latter is interesting from the point of view of discussions upon the drama in general, because it illustrates one of the chief difficulties of the psychological playwright. The first is this. When Hedda tells Tesman that she has destroyed Lövborg's manuscript, and explains (lying, of course) that she did it because she could not bear any one to write better than her husband, she succeeds in preventing him from questioning her, and, indeed, from thinking any more about it, by hinting that she is going to have a child. Tesman at once approaches her with uxorious tenderness, and forgets all about the destruction of a manuscript. Now news of the description Hedda conveys would not drive out of any husband's head the fact that his wife had just burnt a work of genius; but far less out of Tesman's, who was a bookminded man. He prides himself on having proper family feelings; but his heart is in his dog-like reverence for men of intellectual power. It is more probable that he would have exclaimed: "Oh, Hedda, dear, fancy that!" and gone on pressing her with questions and exclaiming about the destruction of Lövborg's book.

The second incident that seems unnatural, is Mrs. Elvsted sitting down with Tesman to reconstruct the book immediately after hearing of Lövborg's death. It is very likely that she should find consolation in this work and marry Tesman over it; but since she was devoted enough to run away from her children and brave a scandal in order to keep an eye on Lövborg while he was under temptation, it is not likely that she would recover in a few minutes from the news of his death. But Ibsen wishes to show the future, and a single incident is all he has time for. Thus, in order to indicate a development psychologically sound, he is driven to represent one of his characters acting in a way which is psychologically false. This is the dilemma that lies in wait for the psychological dramatist at every turn.

How the southern Germans, the mild, reflective *schwärmerish* Germans, who love to drink their yellow wine and brown beer in sunny arbours, who made the songs, and spun the long philosophies, and invented the dusty romance of gigantic erudition, who sit now with melancholy inertia, while unphilosophic, humourless, musicless, pedantic Prussia, with clicking-heels and twitched-up moustachios, stamps romance and individuality out of their country,—how they must have enjoyed the stinging satire of *The Thieves' Comedy!* True, the realism of Frau Wolff's home in the forest, with her hulking husband, and the two frisky young girls, who evidently would rather kiss than spin, may not have been much to their taste; but the egregious Von Wehrhahn, the Emperor-worshipping magistrate, who is so bent on scenting out socialism and sedition that he insults the witnesses and lets thief and receiver escape from under his nose—he must have been a savoury dish!

The satire is delightful to us, who are detached, and the whole play impressively amusing. Miss Filippi acted the part of Frau Wolff, the thieving, indefatigable, imperturbably plausible housewife, extraordinarily well. Who can help liking so cheerful, capable, and sensible a woman? One's sympathies in the matter of the stolen fire-wood and fur coat are violently on her side. Glasenapp (Mr. Norman Page), the old clerk, perched on a high stool in front of an unwieldly ledger, with his plaintive voice and wheedling laughter, faint like the crackle of old parchments, might have come out of or have gone into a novel of Dickens just as he was. *The Thieves' Comedy* is one of those plays that stay in the mind as a series of pictures. Here is one which has kept its colours in mine for two years.

It is quite late, and dark outside the Wolff's cottage. Wulkoff, the barge-man (poacher and receiver as well), has just come in to bargain for a stolen deer. Frau Wolff bustles about her housework as though she did not care two scraps about the matter, repeating her offer in a loud cheerful decided voice, as he climbs sulkily up the ladder of prices. Suddenly a call, melancholy and prolonged like the howl of a dog, is heard outside the window.

"Frau Wolff, Frau Wo-ol-ff." Whist! they stop talking; out goes the light; sack and deer are crammed away; "Frau Wo-o-olf": she goes to the door with an air of astonished cheery welcome, and, after an interval during which a theft of firewood is planned—Mitteldorf, the policeman, comes in! Now no pen can suggest to any one who has not seen Mr. Harry Dodd as Mitteldorf what a smashing anticlimax this is! The hair at the back of your head has been gently raised by that awful tapering cry outside the black window, and by the guilty whispering hurry of the inmates; and then—Mitteldorf appears! Mitteldorf is the stupidest man ever seen on the stage. On this occasion, the night of his understanding is further obscured by a slight haze of beer, and he stidders himself on his heels, for a moment, before stepping in. Frau Wolff is in the habit of selling him a good many of the eggs and other petty filchings, which he spends his days in trying to trace; to-night, he has come in for a chat. I don't think he actually sits down on the deer, and after helping to harness the sleigh, which is destined to carry off the firewood, he goes away.

Not having seen Mr. Harry Dodd in any other parts, I cannot judge the scope of his powers, but his Mitteldorf was the performance of a perfect comedian.

CHAPTER III

Mr. Bernard Shaw

MR. BERNARD SHAW is a difficult subject for criticism: there is so much to discuss, and yet so much has been already said; there are so many interesting things to say about his work which are not quite true, and so many true things which are not interesting; and to crown all, he has explained himself many times. But since his plays are far the most important dramatic contributions the Court Theatre has received, and since its celebrity and success is rooted in them, the critical commentator must give him the largest share of attention. I propose, therefore, in this chapter, to discuss first the characters in these plays; secondly, the treatment of the emotions in them; and thirdly (in the last chapter) to give a separate account of each play and its performance.

HIS CHARACTERS

There is one characteristic of Mr. Shaw's imaginative work which, oddly enough, has not been commented upon; perhaps it has been considered too obvious for comment. It is the exceptional variety and vividness of his characters. They have, too, a peculiar quality, which makes them stay in the memory, and enables them to pass, like the types of Dickens, into conversation. For instance, 'Enery Straker, Prossy, Broadbent, "B. B.," Ann (to rob her of that philosophic universality which her creator claims for her), all possess this quality. Once seen on the stage, they become types in the spectator's imagination, approximations to which he is constantly meeting in real life. Any one, for instance, would be understood directly who said, "I travelled up in the train to-day with a little mechanic—a sort of 'Enery Straker."

Such characters are drawn by constantly bringing into relief one distinguishing feature, too complex perhaps to be defined, in such a way that the imagination instinctively supplies all the other qualities. It is the triumph of the playwright to achieve this intense simplification, and if the Shavian theatre is compared with the work of other modern playwrights in this respect, its superiority is overwhelmingly apparent.

In psychological observation, Mr. Shaw has a caricaturist's quickness in seizing the salient feature; but this is combined in him with a constant sense that the stuff of human nature is much the same in every one. The kind of distinctness which his characters possess differs, consequently, from the distinctness which the old school of psychological dramatists achieved. They were always seeking for "the ruling passion" in their men and women, and making them act accordingly, thus in effect dividing mankind into species—the proud man, the miser, the libertine, etc. Mr. Shaw emphasizes, on the other hand, that men are at bottom swayed by the same common impulses, and that their behaviour is generally what circumstances, education, and the treatment they receive from others at the moment make it; he never fails, therefore, to suggest that society is responsible for their misdeeds as well as for their oddities. As a social reformer, he has theorized upon and analyzed the effect of this or that social environment on life and character; as an artist he has always been preoccupied with human nature. These two preoccupations, working together, have enabled him to seize with extraordinary quickness the traces which a particular manner of living leave on a personality. His figures are often exaggerated; but in nine instances out of ten they are saved from being pointlessly fantastic by the fact that they are closely linked with social conditions. As a propagandist, again, he has perpetually been in violent collision with many people holding different points of view; and as an observer he has noted the particular mental, physical, and social characteristics which usually go with particular ways of looking at the world. Such experience is of the utmost value to the dramatist; for drama depends upon the clash between characters who embody different points of view. If on both sides the difference is one of conflicting desires, that is one kind of drama; but it becomes far more interesting when the opposing wills represent whole groups of ideas by which many men hold and live. Such is the interest of the contest between the poet and the parson, over which Candida stands as umpire; of the discussions between Larry and Broadbent, and of the blind *mêlée* at the end of the play between them and Father Keegan; of the explosive interview between Roebuck and Tanner: of the sharp passage-of-arms between Undershaft and "the honest poor man" Peter Shirley, and of many other spirited encounters. In all these scenes, what impresses us is the hammer-and-tongs vigour with which each combatant stands up for his side, and the natural congruity— not inconsistency, often it is far otherwise—of his outlook with the sort of person his general behaviour shows him to be.

Mr. Shaw is the most striking refutation of the notion that an artist gets the best work out of himself when he holds aloof from the social and religious questions of his day; the artist in him owes an enormous debt to the reformer.

Those characters which strike us as exceptional rather than typical have the same distinctions. Among them Tanner, Valentine, Charteris, and Undershaft are particularly interesting to the analyst, because they combine in varying degrees the temperament and opinions which tell most in Mr. Shaw's writings when he speaks for himself. Tanner and Undershaft have definite systematic views upon morals and politics and human nature; and though Valentine and Charteris have not, they are all four "realists," that is to say, they are not under what Mr. Shaw considers "romantic illusions." Valentine and Charteris would be easy converts to the complete doctrine. Valentine shares the fate of Tanner in being swallowed up in matrimony; but though he betrays a flutter of trepidation before the persistence of the young woman, whose feelings he has just taken by storm, he evidently has never had the true inward horror of his frightful predicament clearly revealed to him. Poor Charteris has even some misgivings about his escape from a similar quandary. It is true there is a touch of irony in his lament upon losing Grace Tranfield, which betrays a glimmering of philosophy;

but there is also more than a trace of regret: Grace Tranfield was not such a one as Ann Whitefield.

"Yes; this is the doom of the philanderer. I shall have to go on philandering now all my life. No domesticity, no fireside, no little ones—nothing at all in Cuthbertson's line." The irony here has two edges.

But there is a second quality common to all these leading characters, unmistakable but harder to describe. It is a temperamental quality, which, by the way, makes these parts extremely hard to act: they are always on the verge of a state of lyrical excitement. Sometimes it takes the form of a sudden towering of high spirits, sometimes of a good-natured combative ecstasy, sometimes of explosive indignation. It differs in each character, but in all it is the same kind of emotion—a sudden sense of freedom and certainty, bringing with it sudden fluency and emphasis of speech, and a feeling of immunity and detachment, which is at the same time a state of extreme emotional mobility. Undershaft takes such moments very solemnly, he is certain he is "saved"; to Valentine they are whiffs of blind exhilarating joy; to the poet in Candida (who has the temperamental quality but does not share the opinions) they are inspirations; to Cusins (who also does not hold them) they are the moments when as a philosophic juggler he can keep all his bowls and basins spinning their fastest, when he can remember the point of twenty creeds at once, and of his love for Barbara into the bargain. To Tanner they are opportunities for psychological declamation.

All authors of merit give to their creations an excess of some characteristic which is dominant in themselves. Thus Mr. Meredith's characters are filled to an unnatural degree with the beauty and courage of life; Balzac gives to his a treble dose of will and appetite; the men and women in Mr. James's novels, the stupid as well as the intelligent, show a far subtler power of perception than such men and women would actually have. In the same way, Mr. Shaw gives to many of his principal characters temperaments which are marked by both extreme mobility and extreme detachment.

Sometimes this gift of himself on the part of a writer is more obviously diffused over the whole of his work than concentrated in characters. *The Tempest*, and, to add a modern example, some of the novels of Mr. Thomas Hardy, are instances. This is what we mean by creating "an atmosphere," when we use that work in a sense of high æsthetic praise, and not simply in order to indicate that the author has succeeded in giving us the sensation of particular scenes or surroundings. In this Mr. Shaw's work (though he is extremely skilful in creating "atmosphere" in the other sense) is deficient, and consequently it is not sufficiently admired by people whose perceptions are quick to see its other merits, but who delight above all things in this quality. His plays, with the exception, perhaps, of *You Never Can Tell*, are the outcome of his imagination working along the lines which his opinions have already laid down, rather than free expressions of his artistic temperament; with the result that those plays are the best to the making of which has gone the most hard, consistent thinking; and those in which the underlying thought is indistinct are, as wholes, very inferior to passages and characters in them—and, indeed, sometimes inferior to the work of inferior writers.

With regard to the characters which are neither "types" nor combinations, in varying proportions, of his own views and temperament, there are two obvious points to notice. Firstly, that all the women are astonishingly real—and how few dramatists can draw more than one kind of woman well! Candida, Nora Reilly, Lady Cecily Waynflete, Mrs. Clandon, Lady Britomart, are as different as possible; yet we know how they would behave under any circumstances. Secondly, the completeness with which such characters as Larry Doyle (a very subtle study), William the waiter, the Rev. James Morell are presented, and the distinctness of such minor figures as Crampton, Mrs. Whitefield, Father Dempsey, Roebuck Ramsden, Barney Doran, Mr. Malone the elder, and Octavius Robinson.

If the reader will review in imagination all the personages mentioned in this section, he will find it hard to parallel in any other dramatist a list of characters so various, so new to the stage, so easy to recognize and to remember.

His Treatment of Emotion

Next to the force with which original characters are presented, the most noticeable feature in Mr. Shaw's work is his treatment of emotion, and especially of sexual emotion. What first strikes us in the Shavian theatre is, perhaps, the frequency of excited scenes, of explosive arguments, violent protestations, gesticulations and agitations. Apart from the frequency of abstract discussions and the vigour of the dialogue there would be nothing very strange in this excitement, were not the passions and emotions, so violently displayed, represented as being also startlingly brief. This emphasis upon brevity of emotions is very characteristic, and one cause of the charge of cynicism which is so often brought against him. The typical scene is one in which the characters are represented in violent states of moral indignation, rage, perplexity, mortification, infatuation, despair, which subside as suddenly as they rise. The Shavian hero is a man who does not take all this hubble-bubble for more than it is worth. He preserves an exasperating good humour through it, however energetic his retorts may be, because he reckons on human nature being moved, in the long run, only by a few fundamental considerations and instincts. The hostility which he excites does not therefore trouble him the least. He counts upon the phenomenon, ultimately working in his favour, that puzzles Tanner in himself when confronted with Ann; that is, upon the contradiction between moral judgments and instinctive likings and respect. Valentine is not dismayed by Gloria's disapproval, nor Bluntschli by Raina's contempt for his lack of conventionally soldier-like qualities; both are confident that the ultimate decisions of these ladies will depend on other things. Even Tanner soon finds himself on excellent terms with Roebuck Ramsden, who began by abusing him as an infamous fellow. But it is not only the fact, that the confidence of the "realists" is always justified in the plays, which emphasizes the instability

of human emotions and judgments; it is one of the fundamental assumptions with regard to human nature which lie
at the back of the plays themselves. It is one of the chief
causes, too, why they are regarded as fantastic; for the
normal instability of emotion has hitherto found very little
reflection in literature or on the stage; vacillations, flaggings,
changes of mind and inconsequences of thought having been
generally confined to characters intended to be obviously weak.
But Mr. Shaw represents, quite truly, characters of considerable firmness in many respects as subject to them.

In common with all writers of comedy he depends for his
effects upon the contradictions between what people say they
believe and how they act; but for his surprises and fun he
draws more than most writers on the normal instability of
feeling.

A great deal of comedy rests upon the weakness of emotions
and aspirations in conflict with the instincts and necessities;
a hungry lover, for instance, thinking more of his breakfast
than his mistress, is a comic figure; so is an indignant
husband being petted into acquiescence. But whether we
laugh happily or not at such scenes, depends upon the spirit
in which they are treated. If this spirit is one of censure
and contempt for the weakness of emotion, the scene becomes
satire at once; but if the scene is presented in such a way
that we recognize the infirmity of human nature, which nevertheless still seems lovable, it remains comedy; and comedy
may include anything from the most boisterous fun to the
tenderest irony. Mr. Shaw's plays are a curious mixture
between comedy and satire. The spirit that prevails in them
is usually one of remorseless scrutiny into the sincerity and
consistency of emotions and motives, and therefore one of
satire; but the severity of the decision in each individual
case is considerably mitigated by the fact that practically
every one else is also found guilty, so that the general impression is that of comedy. He puzzles people by appearing at
the same time very hard on human nature, and very indulgent
to it. His own explanation of the matter is that his ethics
are different from the current morality. He says, in effect,

"If I were to judge you all by the standards your own conscience sets up, which by the bye you are always revoking with extraordinary inconsistency, I should have to condemn you all as more or less worthless; however, I do not judge you according to these principles, but by others of my own." What these are will become clearer when we are examining the plays one by one.

Meanwhile, if "ira" is represented in these plays as a "brevis furor," what is "amor"? In his preface to *Man and Superman,* Mr. Shaw says that "though we have plenty of dramas with heroes and heroines who are in love and must accordingly marry or perish at the end of the play, or about people whose relations with one another have been complicated by the marriage laws, not to mention the looser sort of plays which trade on the tradition that illicit love affairs are at once vicious and delightful, we have no modern English plays in which the natural attraction of the sexes for one another is made the mainspring of the action. . . . What is the usual formula for such plays? A woman has on some past occasion been brought into conflict with the law that regulates the relations of the sexes. A man by falling in love with her, or marrying her, is brought into conflict with the social convention which discountenances the woman. Now the conflicts of individuals with law and convention can be dramatized like all other human conflicts; but they are purely judicial." The reason why such plays are usually so depressing and uninteresting, he argues, is that they are at bottom utterly sexless. We are really more interested in the relations between the man and the woman, which are slurred over, than in the relations between both and the law.

Elsewhere,* however, he has complained that the attraction of the sexes for one another has been made far too much of as "the mainspring of the action"; everything the hero ever does being represented as done for the sake of the woman he loves. His quarrel with modern English dramatists is then, first, that they represent a passion which is only all-powerful

---

*The Preface to *Plays for Puritans.*

in day-dreams as pervasively effective in practical affairs; and secondly, that they do not represent the nature of this passion directly and frankly. His own plays are not open to either objection. In *Man and Superman* he set out purposely to write a play in which sexual attraction should be the main interest; but in his other plays also he has always made the nature of the attraction between his characters quite clear. What is remarkable about the scenes in which this is done, is the extent to which sexual passion is isolated from all other sentiments and emotions. His lovers, instead of using the language of admiration and affection, in which this passion is so often cloaked, simply convey by their words the kind of mental tumult they are in. Sexual attraction is stript bare of all the accessories of poetry and sympathy. It is represented as it is by itself, with its own peculiar romance, but with none of the feelings which may, and often do, accompany it. Take for example the scene between Valentine and Gloria in *You Never Can Tell*.

GLORIA (*uneasily, rising*). Let us go back to the beach.
VALENTINE (*darkly—looking up at her*). What! you feel it too?
GLORIA. Feel what?
VALENTINE. Dread.
GLORIA. Dread!
VALENTINE. As if something were going to happen. It came over me suddenly just before you proposed that we should run away to the others.
GLORIA (*amazed*). That's strange—very strange! I had the same presentiment.
VALENTINE. How extraordinary! (*rising*). Well: shall we run away?
GLORIA. Run away! Oh no: that would be childish. (*She sits down again. He resumes his seat beside her, and watches her with a gravely sympathetic air. She is thoughtful and a little troubled as she adds*) I wonder what is the scientific explanation of those fancies that cross us occasionally!
VALENTINE. Ah, I wonder! It's a curiously helpless sensation: isn't it?
GLORIA. (*rebelling against the word*). Helpless?
VALENTINE. Yes. As if Nature, after allowing us to belong to ourselves and do what we judged right and reasonable for all these years, were suddenly lifting her great hand to take us—her two little children—by the scruffs of our little necks, and use us, in spite of ourselves, for her own purposes, in her own way.

．　．　．　．　．　．　．　．　．

VALENTINE. . . . Oh, I know you mustn't tell me whether you like me or not: but——

GLORIA (*her principles up in arms at once*). *Must* not? Why not? I am a free woman: why should I not tell you?

VALENTINE (*pleading in terror and retreating*). Don't. I'm afraid to hear.

GLORIA (*no longer scornful*). You need not be afraid. I think you are sentimental and a little foolish; but I like you.

VALENTINE (*dropping into the iron chair as if crushed*). Then it's all over. (*He becomes the picture of despair.*)

GLORIA (*puzzled, approaching him*). But why?

VALENTINE. Because liking is not enough. Now that I think down into it seriously, I don't know whether I like you or not.

GLORIA (*looking down at him with wondering concern*). I'm sorry.

VALENTINE (*in an agony of restrained passion*). Oh, don't pity me. Your voice is tearing my heart to pieces. Let me alone, Gloria. You go down into the very depths of me, troubling and stirring me—I can't struggle with it—I can't tell you——

GLORIA (*breaking down suddenly*). Oh, stop telling me what you feel: I can't bear it.

VALENTINE (*springing up triumphantly, the agonized voice now solid, ringing and jubilant*). Ah, it's come at last—my moment of courage. (*He seizes her hands: she looks at him in terror.*) *Our* moment of courage! (*He draws her to him, and kisses her with impetuous strength, and laughs boyishly.*) Now you've done it, Gloria. It's all over: we're in love with one another. (*She can only gasp at him.*) But what a dragon you were! And how hideously afraid I was!

Turn now to the final scene between Ann and Tanner:

TANNER. The will is yours then! The trap was laid from the beginning.

ANN (*concentrating all her magic*). From the beginning—from our childhood—for both of us—by the Life Force.

TANNER. I will not marry you. I will not marry you.

ANN. Oh, you will, you will.

TANNER. I tell you, no, no, no.

ANN. I tell you, yes, yes, yes.

TANNER. No.

ANN (*coaxing—imploring—almost exhausted*). Yes. Before it is too late for repentance. Yes.

TANNER. (*struck by the echo from the past*). When did all this happen to me before? Are we two dreaming?

ANN (*suddenly losing her courage, with an anguish that she does not conceal*). No. We are awake; and you have said no: that is all.

TANNER (*brutally*). Well?

ANN. Well, I made a mistake: you do not love me.

TANNER (*seizing her in his arms*). It is false: I love you. The Life Force enchants me: I have the whole world in my arms when I clasp you. But I am fighting for my freedom, my honor, for my self, one and indivisible.

In both these scenes sexual attraction is isolated and separated from feelings of affection and admiration. The only difference between them is that Tanner struggles to hold himself back and Valentine goes in headlong. The amorous experiences of the Philanderer, of Blanche and Trench (*Widowers' Houses*), of Frank and Vivie (*Mrs. Warren's Profession*) are treated in exactly the same manner; only in these cases the lover does not analyze or understand his own emotion. This emotion must be distinguished from lust on the one hand, and from love on the other; for in the first place, it is imaginative as well as sensual, an excitement of the mind as well as of the body—of the whole living being in fact—and, in the second, it does not include a desire for the other person's welfare, not the conscious contemplation of what is good. Valentine and Tanner know that it is a brief or very intermittent emotion, that it has nothing to do with a perception of the beauty of mind or character; hardly, in Tanner's case, with a perception of bodily beauty: Ann's looks were not the kind of beauty which signified much to him. Like his prototype Don Juan when in love, his ear and eye probably tore her voice and looks to pieces; like him he could say, "My judgment was not corrupted: my brain still said no on every issue. And whilst I was in the act of framing my excuses to the lady, Life seized me and threw me into her arms as a sailor throws a scrap of fish into the mouth of a sea-bird."[1]

The merit of all these scenes is that they convey with perfect clearness the emotion which possesses the characters so that it is recognized at once as a real one, and one which has been sentimentally identified with other emotions to the devastation of literature and the confusion of life. The artistic merit of such work requires no comment, and its social

---

[1] *Don Juan in Hell* (Act III. of *Man and Superman* as published).

importance lies in helping people to distinguish better between their emotions and therefore to walk more surefootedly through life. But at this point Mr. Shaw's peculiar bias comes in. His principal intellectual failing, so it seems to me, is to exaggerate the stupidity of mankind. No other writer, not even Carlyle or Tolstoi, appears so convinced that the mistakes and confusions of thought, of which men are guilty, are an absurd, glaring, staring set of elementary blunders. So with regard to the emotion of love, he says in so many words—"You have idealized and sentimentalized love. I will show you what that emotion is. Come, rub your eyes; look at it; isn't that what you mean by being in love? Have you the folly to say now that it is worth more than anything else in the world?" And we look, and admit we have often called precisely that emotion "being in love," and that it was never better represented; but we feel, especially now we see it so clearly, it was not *that* emotion after all to which we gave such importance, but that there is still something very difficult to define to which this value justly belongs. Nor do we mean then by love the impartial sympathy and kindness which Lady Cecily Waynflete feels towards every one she meets; that is a rare and beautiful quality, and very romantic when it is so constant as it is in her, but that is not it. What Cusins is indicated as feeling in *Major Barbara* is much more like it; but notice now where Mr. Shaw's bias comes in. He sums up Cusins's feelings for Barbara by saying, "By the operation of some instinct which is not merciful enough to blind him with the illusions of love, he is obstinately bent on marrying her." As an artist, he has put into their behaviour together a great deal more than this; but as a writer of analytical stage-directions and philosophic prefaces, he will not admit that it is more than a case of Tanner and Ann or Valentine and Gloria over again. It is perfectly clear that Cusins, while as a critical observer he may be quite aware of Barbara's faults, and while he is attracted to her instinctively, also feels that happiness in the contemplation of her mind and character and the expression of them in her person, which is included in the common conception of love. But Mr. Shaw's contempt for the shoddy confusions of passionate literature, his knowledge of the ease with which men deceive themselves at these junctures, and his constant prejudice that the ordinary view must be hopelessly beside the point, lead him as a philosophical critic to ignore emotional complications, which as an artist he here reflects in his work; and these complications, carried vaguely in the ordinary man's mind, prevent him from being satisfied by Mr. Shaw's demonstration that love between the sexes has little or no value in itself, and no significance except as a trustworthy indication that the offspring of that particular union are likely to be sound.

I have discussed the treatment of the emotions as exhibited in these plays at some length, and especially those of love and sexual attraction; because one general impression which Mr. Shaw's work leaves behind is that of a loveless world in which actions, which seem the result of affection, are explained as having other causes. On nearer inspection this impression appears to be due to the natural trend of his powers rather than to limitations of feeling. His mission is not to glorify what is best in human nature, but to make men scrutinize their pretensions, their emotions, and their conscience. He satirizes rather their virtues and the emotions of which they are proud than the faults to which they would cry "peccavi." But he is apt to weaken his case by ignoring the sound element in the emotions and qualities he attacks, and sometimes we find him honouring in one place the very quality he attacked elsewhere as a vice masquerading as a virtue. For instance, he attacks (in *Major Barbara*) the emotion of sympathy for suffering and helplessness which he honours in *Captain Brassbound's Conversion*. Perhaps he would say that Barbara and Lady Cecily did not feel pity; but without compassion, their kindness would have been more patronizing and less effectual than the sentimental pity he detests as insufferably morbid and condescending. Again, he jeers at unselfishness, exhorting every man to fight for his own hand irrespective of consequences to others in the one play; and in the other he explains the secret of power as a forgetfulness of self. True, the unselfishness he attacks is part humbug and part feebleness, the kind which make a person a nuisance by compelling all who have to do with him to look after his interests as well as their own; and what Mr. Shaw means is simply that you must help yourself, if you are to help others. But he does not give his fellow-men the credit for seeing these distinctions, and he thinks apparently that they will only take the lesson if he ignores them himself for the sake of emphasis. He asserts that forgiveness is a disastrous principle, and in the same book advocates that very man, whatever he may have done, should have the chance of being treated as though he were still capable of decent conduct and feelings, which is the essence of forgiveness. He pours contempt on humility as a kind of perverted emotional luxury or shirking, and yet one of the qualities for which he shows most sympathy is the sense of proportion that makes a man consider his own emotional struggles and catastrophes, or even his own moral progress and refinement, as after all of small consequence compared to the total effect of his conduct in a world bursting with misery. What is this if it is not humility? These contradictions do not spring from a confused view of life; but from the persuasion that he is writing for a world of fools, who are so dense and inert, that they can only be startled into attention; who, being incapable of keeping separate things distinct, are also incapable of being moved by anything but emphatic one-sided statement. It is this conviction which mars much of his work; for it is not true. The ordinary man feels many more distinctions than he can express. Though he may be unable always to refute Mr. Shaw, he does feel that a great many important things have been left out in dealing with human nature and society, and therefore he is inclined to ignore him as a maker of paradoxes, or merely to enjoy him as a wit. If Mr. Shaw had felt more constantly the truth of his own maxim: "The difference between the shallowest routiner and the deepest thinker appears, to the latter, trifling; to the former, infinite"—for presumably the thinker sees the truth in this matter also: better than the ordinary man—his work would have been more convincing. Nevertheless, the influence of clearness and emphatic presentation, and of a point of view extremely well stated, must always be wide. It is a great thing to have a side of things so vividly expressed that you can turn to the author at any time in confidence that you will find in him its most absolute and forcible expression. It is one of the chief causes of lasting reputation. As to Mr. Shaw's influence upon his contemporaries, this is best measured by noting how frequently in reading or talking you come across a view of things, which makes you think, "I wonder whether that is derived from Bernard Shaw"; or by a still subtler test, by watching how often in your private ruminations upon some experience or other the suggestion crosses your mind, "Was my view of my own feelings coloured by such and such a scene in Shaw's plays or novels?" You may say "Yes—and a reason for distrusting it;" but whether you say that, or whether you marvel at his insight, the fact that the idea occurs at all is a sign that he is an author of real significance.

CHAPTER IV

The Shaw Plays and Performances

CANDIDA

CANDIDA was first produced at the Court Theatre on April 26, 1904. Miss Janet Achurch and Mr. Charrington had taken it round the provinces some years before. The most striking feature in the Court performance was Mr. Granville Barker's acting of the poet, Eugene Marchbanks; excepting this, and the acting of Miss Sydney Fairbrother, who represented perfectly the pert, self-respecting honesty and suppressed sentimental devotion of the little cockney typist, it was not better than the earlier rendering.

Candida is the story of the love of a poet, age eighteen for a practical, clear-headed, sympathetic woman, who has been married some years to a hard-working, socialistic clergyman, with a tremendous gift for moral exhortation. He is a perfectly sincere man, in the sense that he has never uttered a word which he did not honestly believe to be sincere at the time. But in order to get the maximum energy out of himself he has avoided probing himself or examining his relations towards others. His habitual behaviour and utterances would come therefore under the head of what Carlyle called "sincere cant." He is certainly a good man, and believes himself to be a strong one. He is devoted to his wife, who returns his affection; but he regards himself as her protector, and the adoration with which his fellow-workers look up to him, and the influence he wields from the platform and pulpit have blinded him to the fact that he is really the weaker of the two. She, on the other hand, is well aware of this, and it increases her love for him to feel he needs her help.

Into this household comes the poet, who is so sensitive to the attitudes of the people towards him and the emotional atmosphere of the moment, that he is almost helpless in practical matters. He is a shrinking, embarrassed creature, who appeals to Candida's tenderness at first as an adorer, whom she can shelter and protect. But she soon becomes aware of a side of him which goes near to alarming her once or twice, just as it disturbs poor "Prossy," and ends by terrifying Morell. In fact, it would frighten her too, were she not at bottom the most matter-of-fact of the four. Candida has a good deal of George Sand in her. She has a great admiration for intense emotion and poetic sensibility; but you feel that the only things she really believes in are the obvious things, which plain people value most, a happy fireside, hard regular work and practical kindness. There is, really, no plumbing the depths of her condescension towards the ideals of a poet. Marchbanks appeals to her as Chopin and De Musset appealed to George Sand; while thinking that she sympathizes with him completely, she really only sympathizes in so far as she can mother and comfort him. Nevertheless, she is immensely grateful to him for understanding her situation, and enjoys his adoration without being moved by it. She realizes at the end that he must stand alone; for, like all true poets, he is incorruptibly sincere and courageous in facing the extent of his longings, and he will not allow them to be satisfied with less than ambrosial food. Living in a world of emotions, and understanding them, he is strong when others are weak. The Rev. James Morell begins by launching patronizingly at what he considers a case of calf-love—and, too, he feels so sure of Candida. The dialogue between them is one of the truest and most spirited Mr. Shaw has written. It is magnificent.

Morell rapidly begins to realize that this love is something more serious than he expected; and still sonorously self-complacent, though keeping up with more and more difficulty an attitude of brotherly forbearance, he proceeds to crush the poet with lofty reproaches and moral harangues, which, alas, have a fatal platform ring about them. They are powerful enough in their way (Mr. Shaw does not secure the poet's victory by undermining his adversary beforehand), but they are nothing to the terrible directness of Marchbanks's retorts. Every one makes a breach in the parson's self-confidence which hitherto he thought justly based and impregnable. But his habit of attacking others from the pulpit has unfitted him for a close-quarters grapple with an adversary whose sincerity is profounder than his own. He begins to feel his own weakness, and the fear seizes him that perhaps the poet is right, and that when rousing meetings to enthusiasm by his emotional oratory his wife may have despised him in her heart. He loses self-control and shakes Marchbanks by the collar, who screams in nervous terror.

MARCHBANKS. . . . (*Morell grasps him powerfully by the lapel of his coat: he cowers down on the sofa and screams passionately.*) Stop, Morell: if you strike me I'll kill myself: I won't bear it (*almost in hysterics.*) Let me go. Take your hand away.

MORELL (*with slow emphatic scorn*). You little snivelling cowardly whelp. (*He releases him.*) Go, before you frighten yourself into a fit.

MARCHBANKS (*on the sofa, but relieved by the withdrawal of Morell's hand*). I'm not afraid of you: it's you who are afraid of me.

MORELL (*quietly, as he stands over him*). It looks like it, doesn't it?

MARCHBANKS (*with petulant vehemence*). Yes, it does. (*Morell turns away contemptuously. Eugene scrambles to his feet and follows him.*) You think because I shrink from being brutally handled—because (*with tears in his voice*) I can do nothing but cry with rage when I am met with violence—because I can't lift a heavy trunk down from the top of a cab like you—because I can't fight you for your wife as a navvy would: all that makes you think I am afraid of you. But you're wrong. If I haven't got what you call British pluck, I haven't British cowardice either: I'm not afraid of a clergyman's ideas. I'll fight your ideas. I'll rescue her from her slavery to them: I'll pit my own ideas against them. You are driving me out of the house because you daren't let her choose between your ideas and mine. You are afraid to let me see her again. (*Morell, angered, turns suddenly on him. He flies to the door in involuntary dread.*) Let me alone, I say. I'm going.

MORELL (*with cold scorn*). Wait a moment. I'm not going to touch you: don't be afraid. When my wife comes back she will want to know why you have gone. And when she finds that you are never going to cross our threshold again, she will want to have that explained too. Now I don't wish to distress her by telling her that you have behaved like a blackguard.

MARCHBANKS (*coming back with renewed vehemence*). You shall—you must. If you give any explanation but the true one, you are a liar and a coward. Tell her what I said; and how you were strong and manly, and shook me as a terrier shakes a rat; and how I shrank and was terrified; and how you called me a snivelling little whelp and put me out of the house. If you don't tell, I will: I'll write it to her.

MORELL (*taken aback*). Why do you want her to know this?

MARCHBANKS (*with lyric rapture*). Because she will understand me, and know that I understand her. If you keep back one word of it from her—if you are not ready to lay the truth at her feet as I am—then you will know to the end of your days that she really belongs to me and not to you. Good-bye.

MORELL (*terribly disquieted*). Stop: I will not tell her.

MARCHBANKS (*turning near the door*). Either the truth or a lie you *must* tell her if I go.

MORELL (*temporizing*). Marchbanks: it is sometimes justifiable——

MARCHBANKS (*cutting him short*). I know—to lie. It will be useless. Good-bye, Mr. Clergyman. (*As he turns finally to the door, it opens, and Candida enters in her housekeeping dress.*)

There are no explanations for the present. In the last act Morell and the poet confront her together, and demand that she shall choose between them. Candida with ironical acquiescence consents, and proposes that they should make their bids for her. Her husband in the vein of proud, manly humility offers her his strength for her protection, his honesty of purpose for her surety, his industry for her living, etc.

CANDIDA (*quite quietly*). And you, Eugene? What do you offer?

MARCHBANKS. My weakness! my desolation! my heart's need!

CANDIDA. That's a good bid, Eugene. Now I know how to make my choice——

and she chooses "the weaker." Morell collapses, thinking it is all over, but the poet knows in a moment that the sentence has gone against him.

The play ends with an explanation from Candida why Morell is weak and Eugene strong. The poet goes away without bitterness, and husband and wife fall into each other's arms. But, we are told, neither of them knows the secret which is in the poet's heart. This secret, however, is easy to divine; it is the knowledge that the love which those two have for each other is not what he wants or envies, or, to put it prosaically, it is a contempt for roseate domesticity.

The play is among the best Mr. Shaw has written. The interest is concentrated on the main theme throughout, and it finishes at the point from which the audience, looking back, can best understand all that has happened, which cannot be said of his last two plays. It is the first play to show what is becoming more and more obvious in his writings, that, in addition to the rationalistic point of view from which he criticizes conventions and social institutions, he looks on the world from another, which is defiantly and ruthlessly idealistic. As a socialist, he is always attempting to prove that social and moral conventions must be broken up and changed because they do not lead to human happiness; but his favourable judgment of individuals depends upon the extent to which they despise and dispense with happiness themselves. In personal relations, in love, he apparently see little value; love is a comfort, a consoling kind of happiness, which a great man can do without; when he is tired and discouraged he may crave for it; but these are his feebler moments. At his best he is self-sufficient; content in the place of happiness with a kind of occasional triumphant gaiety, springing from a sense of his own fortitude and power. In the later plays which we shall examine, we shall find him recognizing this as fundamentally a religious emotion, and trying to find the view of the universe which justifies and explains it. Meanwhile it is worth noting that the poet is the first character of this kind, who is used as a touchstone to test the metal of the others. Mr. Granville Barker succeeded in playing Eugene Marchbanks where almost every other actor would have failed, because the representation of a lyrical mood is one within the peculiar range of his powers. His voice, too, can express a contemplative ecstasy. It possesses a curious individual quality, which, while it limits the range of his impersonations, gives particular intensity to some. When he repeats her name "Candida, Candida, Candida," there is not a touch of self-consciousness in the musical reiteration; he does not appear to be following the sound of his own voice like most actors at such times, but to be listening, detached, to his longing made audible.

It is in his representation of intellectual emotions that he excels, and so he excels in this part. Miss Kate Rorke was Candida to perfection in her capacity, promptitude, width of mind and patronage and kindliness; but she left out Candida's smiles, her irony, her maternity, and the *charm* of her perfect self-control. Mr. C. V. France (I did not see Mr. McKinnel) as James Morell did not give sufficiently the impression of a character with a large emotional surface. Morell's thoughtfulness for others, too, though it had become largely a mechanical habit, must have always had more of the actor's perennial impetuousity about it. Nor did Mr. France give the impression of a man who is readily excited by his own words and attitudes, which Morell the orator certainly was. His performance as the parson in *The Convict on the Hearth* was a better one, though his Morell was far from being insignificant.

JOHN BULL'S OTHER ISLAND

If *Candida* is one of the best of Mr. Shaw's plays for the completeness with which it contains and finishes its story, *John Bull's Other Island* is remarkable for being equally successful for entirely different reasons. It is a play with hardly any story, with no climax, without the vestige of a plot, and without anything like an ending, in fact without one of the qualities of the "well-constructed" play; yet it is nevertheless an absolute success. The story is simply that of two friends and partners, an Irishman and an Englishman, who visit the former's old home in order to foreclose a mortgage. Incidentally, the Englishman determines to stand for the local seat, and becomes engaged, with his friend's approval, to a young woman with whom the latter had been on rather romantic terms for a short time before starting on his career. That is all: could anything sound more unpromising? There is not even a touch of jealousy to offer a chance for dramatic effect. The interest lies solely in the presentation of character and in the contrast between temperaments; but this is achieved in a masterly fashion. The play has the one æsthetic technical quality, which is necessary to its perfection; the characters are developed by means of a perfectly natural sequence of events; there is no appearance of circumstances being created for the sake of exhibiting them; everything that happens has the air of happening by chance.

Every critic of this play must stop on the threshold of his comments to remark, with whatever emphasis he can command, that the performance itself was one of the best ever given in London. There were faults, of course, but they are only worth mentioning, if this fact is remembered.

Mr. Shaw has explained in his preface to the play what he conceives to be the main difference between the Englishman and the Irishman. The Irishman is more imaginative, but he has no illusions about matters of fact; while the Englishman is at the mercy of such imagination as he possesses, and has in consequence a confused sentimental conception of reality. The Duke of Wellington, according to him, is a typical Irishman, while Nelson is typically English. This difference in temperament he attributes not to race (he does not believe in race) but to the climate. These discussions about national characteristics make very good conversation, but it is hard to feel satisfied with the conclusions; for the exceptions are too numerous. For instance, according to Mr. Shaw's theory, you would expect to find that such Englishmen as Fielding, Defoe, Cobbett, Gissing, Samuel Butler, had been brought up in the soft moist air and among the brown bogs and heather of Rosscullen, and that such Irishmen as Goldsmith and Steele, who were so full of romantic sentiment about actualities and dearly loved a fool (which Mr. Shaw says is almost impossible for an Irishman) had never even been to Ireland. But whether the theory propounded in the preface is true or not, in the play Larry Doyle and Broadbent are extraordinarily vivid characters, who recall familiar types of Irishmen and Englishmen. The contrast between the two is most striking at the following points. Broadbent is full of "heart," and takes himself and everything he does and every one he meets absolutely seriously; he has no sense of humour, or of refinement, or of proportion. Larry is discriminative to the point of chilly fastidiousness; he cannot enjoy life and he cannot idealize any human being: he cannot love, though he is fond of Tom Broadbent because

Tom's warmth of emotion helps him to feel things are worth while at the moment, and because his nature is essentially practical and active, while Larry himself is only capable of being moved by ideals in which he does not believe. He is exasperated by this tendency in himself to feel only the beauty and significance of things which do not exist in any satisfying quantities; hence the bitterness of his contempt for romance and mysticism. His life is a perpetual struggle to get used to the world; it is a point of pride with him not to feel an exile here; hence his enthusiasm for the big international world of shipping, engineering and business, into which he has escaped from his dreams and thoughts in poverty-stricken Rosscullen. But business does not really fill him with enthusiasm, and he knows it; hence his fierce dislike of Father Keegan, who, with the same heart-sickness in him, has taken the opposite course, and turned away from reality to live in contemplation of a far-off perfection. Larry feels, as keenly as Father Keegan, the futility and vulgarity of Broadbent's schemes; but he fights fiercely for them because anything seems more tolerable than the helplessness of a visionary's protest against the world.

Mr. J. L. Shine's Larry was not so good as many of the other parts; but he did give the impression of loneliness and distraction of heart and of perpetual tension of will to keep turned towards one path in life, which are far the most important characteristics to represent in Larry.

Broadbent, on the other hand, talks with the most reverential enthusiasm of Ruskin and Shelley (whose works he was very fond of reading, he says, as a boy), and he listens in the same spirit to the discourses of Keegan; but there is a profounder disrespect implied in his admiration than in Larry's impatience; for Broadbent is absolutely incapable of really believing in such things; the works of Ruskin and Shelley are merely pots of romantic paint to him, wherein he finds colours with which to daub his own undertakings.

Mr. Louis Calvert's Broadbent was a masterpiece of acting. It is seldom that a character so thoroughly homogeneous in gesture, voice, and carriage is seen on the stage. Mr. Shaw's description of him runs as follows: "a robust, full-blooded, energetic man in the prime of life, sometimes eager and credulous, sometimes shrewd and roguish, sometimes portentously solemn, sometimes jolly and impetuous, always buoyant and irresistible, mostly likable; and enormously absurd in his most earnest moments." Mr. Calvert was all this to the life. The meeting between Broadbent and Nora Reilly by the round tower, on the first night of his arrival at Rosscullen, when his romantic feelings are so strange to himself, that he accepts Nora's suggestion he is drunk, with shame and conviction, is a delicious bit of comedy. His subsequent wooing of Nora and his easy triumph was a painful spectacle, for Nora is a charming person; but the scene is distressingly plausible.

Mr. Barker as Father Keegan did not quite succeed in inspiring the sense of remote dignity which it is important to emphasize in contrast to the eupeptic irreverence of Broadbent and to the squalid go-as-you-please Irish characters. How good they all were! Corney Doyle (Mr. F. Cremlin) with his drawling manner and calculating eye; Father Dempsey (Mr. Beveridge) with unction, authority, and familiarity so perfectly blended in his manner; Barney Doran (Mr. Wilfred Shine), the clever sloven with plenty of heartiness and no heart; and Mat Haffigan (Mr. A. E. George), that gnarled old stump of dogged density! Miss Ellen O'Malley's Nora had a genuine poetic charm, a quality which hardly ever crosses the footlights.

YOU NEVER CAN TELL

The story of this play is so small a part of it, that it is not worth while telling; the interest lies entirely in the characters. *You Never Can Tell* has proved one of the most popular of Mr. Shaw's plays, partly because its peculiar wit and high spirits communicate to the spectator's mind a kind of dancing freedom; and partly because the criticism in it upon social distinctions, the family, and the conventions of courtship, instead of being hurled in truculent harangues across the foot-lights, is conveyed indirectly during the course of the story—and, lastly, because the whole play is tinged with the serene resignation of the gentle refrain, "You never can tell, sir, you never can tell."

Connoisseurs are tiresome with their definitions of true comedy, when the upshot of them is that nothing can be comedy unless it is very like what has already been written. Mr. Shaw's plays may or may not be comedy; their pervading spirit is certainly rather one of scrutiny than of indulgence, and humanity on his stage is always under the stare of a terrible eye; but whether the presence of these qualities in his work settle the question or not, it is clear that *You Never Can Tell* approaches more nearly than the others to what every one considers comedy.

How delightful is William the waiter! The "silky old man, white-haired and delicate looking, but so cheerful and contented that in his encouraging presence ambition stands rebuked as vulgarity and imagination as treason to the abounding sufficiency and interest of the actual." How beautifully Mr. Calvert played him! He gathered the teacups with the tenderness of a lady picking flowers in her garden; he proffered coats and parasols with a concern untouched by servility, but profoundly absurd; his voice was like oil on troubled waters; he was the personification of that sense of the importance of the moment, which, emphasized, is the source of the most delicious irony. What a dissertation might be written upon William! William the leveller, William the impassive, William the imperturbably, universally kind! His kinship to Mother Earth might be shown; he might be compared to the over-arching blue, which dwarfs frantic gesticulations and is no sounding-board for violent declaimers. One cannot help regretting that his spirit does not more often brood over the plays of Mr. Shaw.

The love interest in this play has already been discussed in connection with Mr. Shaw's general treatment of that theme; but it is worth while insisting again upon its main feature. Love appears as an impulse which cannot be rationalized, only explained. The state of falling in love is, according to this theory, one that a clear-headed man will recognize as a kind of dream, in which individuals have a value his wide-awake judgment would never allow them. That is to say, it makes complete nonsense of life. In his later plays Mr. Shaw justifies it on the ground of a faith in the purposes of nature, of "the Life Force"; in this one, Valentine, unlike Tanner who philosophizes upon it, recklessly enjoys its exhilaration, though he knows it may land him where he has no wish to be. When Gloria, like Ann, turns round to hold her lover, who when it comes to the point would be half glad to get off, it was curious to note that the audience always roared with laughter, just as they did at the tremendous moment in the last act of *Man and Superman*. If this jars on those who see the serious intention of the author, how trying it must be to the actors themselves.

The Twins, who are so delightful to the reader, never quite came up to expectation on the stage. High spirits and spontaneous fun are extraordinarily difficult to act; especially when they take the form of a boyish burlesque of sententiousness. The Twins are always acting up to a comic conception of themselves; it is very hard for the actors to represent two young creatures doing this *naturally*. The fault I had to find with the playing of Miss Dorothy Minto and Mr. Page is that they did not always exhibit enough the physical signs of the animal spirits which prompt their irrepressible comments. The rollicking tirades about their twentieth-century mother and Gloria, in the first act, did not quite come off for this reason. In Miss Minto, who was so admirable in the quarrel with her father, I missed the flash of teeth and eyes in smiling, which I imagine to have been one of the characteristics which made the assaults of the real Dolly so flabbergasting; but when she was momentarily suppressed she was excellent. Mr. Page often lacked vivacity. But certainly this want is better than the over-acting the part easily invites.

Miss Watson brought out the unamiable platform side of Mrs. Clandon. You could imagine how carefully just she always tried to be to her children; but you missed the indulgent generous quality in her, which was so remarkable in Mrs. Wright's impersonation, making the family much more conceivable as a family, and Mrs. Clandon's implacable attitude to her husband much more interesting. Owing to this peculiarity in Miss Watson's finished acting, the scene in which the Twins, after trying to get out of their mother the name of their father, go over to her side against Gloria, did not seem significant.

Mr. Edmund Gurney, as Crampton, cut as unamiably grotesque a figure as he ought. He was wonderfully unattractive, and, when he climbed down and dropped the domineering father, like all unattractive cross-grained people trying to conciliate affection, he became pitiable. There was real pathos in the pleading glances of his dazed and choleric little eye, in the movements of his mouth, as though he found consideration for others a bitter draught, and in the clumsy, checked gestures of his tenderness. Mr. James Hearn as Bohun used a fine hectoring voice; but he emphasized already too frequent repetitions of his part by a monotonous shaking of his finger at the individual to be put down.

The part of Valentine was played on different occasions by Mr. Granville Barker and Mr. Ainley. The latter's was a very fair performance, but he did not express well the gaiety and violence which are part of Valentine's character. Where Mr. Barker excelled was precisely in those brisk leaps of the heart, which are so characteristic of Mr. Shaw's lovers; for instance, in such a passage as this, at the end of an interview during which Gloria has been very scornful.

VALENTINE. Love can't give any man new gifts. It can only heighten the gifts he was born with.
GLORIA. What gifts were you born with, pray?
VALENTINE. Lightness of heart.
GLORIA. And lightness of head, and lightness of faith, and lightness of everything that makes a man.
VALENTINE. Yes, the whole world is like a feather dancing in the light now, and Gloria is the sun. I beg your pardon; I'm off. Back at nine. Good-bye.

Mr. Barnes' Finch McComas was a most delightful piece of comedy. Finch in his youth was an ardent reformer; when he appears on the stage he is an eminently respectful solicitor.

His character bears some analogy to Roebuck Ramsden; they are both 1860 types, only Finch is well aware that his ideas are no longer advanced. He informs Mr. Clandon, newly arrived from Madeira, that the ideas they upheld together in their youth, for which she is still strenuously prepared to suffer social ostracism, are now perfectly respectable; in fact, that they might be professed by any bishop; only in one place could they possibly be considered as advanced—in the theatre.

MAN AND SUPERMAN

This play is a tragi-comic love-chase of a man by a woman. It is based on the philosophy of sex already discussed, with this corollary added: that in such matters the woman is always the pursuer, and man the pursued: a corollary obviously untrue, which gains, however, a certain plausibility of appeal both from the fact, which everybody knows though it is sometimes conventionally concealed, that women take love-likings as often as men, and in their own ways seek as often to attain their object, and also from the experience of men who have made love and run away, that the women not unnaturally sometimes run after them. But if the case of Ann and Tanner is taken as an individual case, which it becomes when shorn of preface and appendices on the stage, the general significance which the author attributes to it need not annoy us. The play is the most *brilliant* piece of work Mr. Shaw has done.

Ann is "Everywoman" according to Mr. Shaw's philosophy; though every woman is not Ann. As an individual character she is excellent. Her instinct leads her to mark down Tanner as the father for her children. He knows that marriage means loss of liberty, and therefore of efficiency and happiness. He has no respect for Ann's character, and he only approves of her as a philosopher because all impulses, actions and thoughts are subordinated in her to nature's vital purpose.

Jack Tanner, with his explosions of nervous energy and exasperated eloquence, is as good as Ann. The contrasting male character is the poetical, chivalrous, romantic Octavius.

He woos Ann, who would never be willing to take him as a husband; for the poetic temperament is barren, "the Life Force passes it by." Marriage, if he only knew, would be equally fatal to him; for his goddess, his inspiration, would vanish in the real "flesh and blood" woman and mother, who is not lovable in herself and in so far as she is "woman" (and Ann is little else) can only really care for her children. Tanner in the end, as Don Juan explains of himself in the dream, yields because he cannot help it. He despises Ann; she is bully and liar, "and unscrupulously uses her personal fascinations to make men give her what she wants, which makes her something for which there is no polite name." She will think his aspirations and efforts to reform society absurd, and thwart him as much as she dares; and, above all, she is a hypocrite. But though Tanner surrenders reluctantly he gives in at last with a good conscience; for Ann and he, in submitting to their attraction for each other, become the servants of "the Life Force," or will of the world. Henceforth they are instruments to the creation of the Superman, which is the only aim worth working for in this world; and they are both right to sacrifice, she her happiness and perhaps her life, he his happiness and aims and generous ambitions; for such things cannot compare in importance with the bringing into the world of children, born of mutual attraction. But the institution which compels two people who have nothing in common, saving this impulse towards each other, to spend their two lives together, is iniquitous. The conclusion which logically follows from the assertion that the child is the sole end of marriage, is that it is absurd to make marriage binding. Moreover, the consideration that the rest of life will have to be spent together induces men and women to marry for irrelevant reasons, such as affection or self-interest, to the detriment of subsequent generations. That is the moral of a comedy which keeps many people laughing, who would not laugh if they understood.

Mr. Granville Barker's Tanner was one of his best parts. It was a pity perhaps that he did not make Tanner seem more formidable. Ann's cool audacity and insidious perseverance were admirable, but Miss McCarthy missed one point in the character. Ann after all had some fun in her; it was perhaps her only redeeming quality from an ordinary point of view; Miss McCarthy did not suggest this. Mr. Casson as Octavius was finely insignificant. The whole performance was extraordinarily good. Miss Florence Haydon as Mrs. Whitefield and Mr. Gwenn as Straker have identified themselves for ever in these characters in our imaginations. Miss Sarah Brooke as that hard, competent, pretty young woman, Violet Robinson, Mr. Barnes as Roebuck Ramsden, and Miss Agnes Thomas as an acid old maid, all reached that pitch of excellence in their parts which makes a living person start up before the mind's eye afterwards, whenever the name of the character is mentioned.

CAPTAIN BRASSBOUND'S CONVERSION

The moral of this play is that revenge is silly and vulgar, and justice with retaliatory punishments is only a wilder kind of revenge. Lady Cecily Waynflete manages and keeps in perfect order the horde of ramshackle banditti, amongst whom she and her brother find themselves, by ignoring their dangerous intentions as childish naughtinesses, and treated every one of them as though they were amiable fellows. Her power springs from absolute fearlessness and a most kindly sympathy, which is not in her an irregular or interrupted impulse, but a constant feeling. She is a gentle, humorous, cheerful, naturally domesticated person, but a very persistent immovable one. To borrow a metaphor, there is in her nature a quality which answers to the fly-wheel in a mill, which distributes the motion equally over all the wheels. She is always telling people what pleasant faces they have and how much she likes them; and this is how she genuinely feels towards all she meets. The story runs as follows: Sir Howard Hallam, one of His Majesty's judges, and Lady Cecily, his sister-in-law, are taking a holiday tour in Morocco. They are anxious to make an expedition into the interior, a tract of country which is dangerous to Christian travellers, owing to the fanaticism of the Mohammedan tribes. A certain Captain Brassbound, who carries on a dubious coasting trade (really smuggling and piracy), sometimes provides an escort for tourists in this district. In spite of the warnings of the missionary at the coast town, they determine to trust him; though Lady Cecily is, of course, reluctant to have an escort at all; such men, she says, always want such a lot of looking after. However, Sir Howard and the missionary are firm on this point, and she resigns herself. She is not the least alarmed when she hears that every native believes that he will go to heaven if he kills an unbeliever, and replies with point, "Bless you, dear Mr. Rankin, the people in England believe that they will go to heaven if they give all their property to the poor. But they don't do it. I'm not a bit afraid of that."

Now Brassbound is really the son of Sir Howard's brother. His mother was a drunken half-crazy woman, who after her husband's death pestered the judge, her brother-in-law, to such an extent that he had an order of restraint made out against her. There was a piece of property, too, in Jamaica, over which there was a long legal dispute; it is now in the judge's hands. The upshot of all this, as far as concerns the position of the characters at the beginning of the play, is that Captain Brassbound, alias "Black Paquito," has been nursing for years a romantic hatred of his uncle, as the murderer and robber of his mother; Sir Howard, of course, never dreams of the relationship between them. It is the captain's intention to revenge his mother by delivering the travellers over to the mercy of the fanatic, Sidi el Assif. But his whole romantic scheme of revenge collapses on closer acquaintance with Lady Cecily. He clings to it desperately because he has invested all his self-respect in the idea that he is a wronged man, who has a great act of reparative justice to perform; but it is no use; her kindliness, perfect good faith, and good sense, take the life out of his revenge. He begins by resenting and repulsing her kind actions towards himself and his men; but these are so practical, and are done in so amiable a spirit that he cannot hold out long. There is an explosive scene, of course, between Captain Brassbound and Sir Howard, when the former declares his relationship and resolve, in which Sir Howard speaks up stoutly, declaring that Brassbound may do his worst, but that he and the rest of his gang shall certainly swing for it, while Lady Cecily sits by rather distressed, but quite calm. After this scene follows a dialogue between her and Captain Brassbound, so typical of the delightful serious comedy of the whole play that it must be quoted.

BRASSBOUND. Don't quibble with me. I am going to do my duty as a son; and you know it.

LADY CECILY. But I should have thought the time for that was in your mother's lifetime, when you could have been kind and forbearing with her. Hurting your uncle won't do her any good, you know.

BRASSBOUND. It will teach other scoundrels to respect widows and orphans. Do you forget that there is such a thing as justice?

LADE CECILY (*gaily shaking out the finished coat*). Oh, if you are going to dress yourself in ermine and call yourself Justice, I give you up. You are just your uncle over again; only he gets £5000 a year for it, and you do it for nothing. (*She holds the coat up to see if any further repairs are needed.*)

BRASSBOUND (*sulkily*). You twist my words very cleverly. But no man or woman has ever changed me.

LADY CECILY. Dear me! That must be very nice for the people you deal with, because they can always depend on you; but isn't it rather inconvenient for yourself when you change your mind?

BRASSBOUND. I never change my mind.

LADY CECILY (*rising with the coat in her hands*). Oh! oh! Nothing will ever persuade me that you are as pigheaded as that.

BRASSBOUND. (*offended*). Pigheaded!

LADY CECILY (*with quick, caressing apology*). No, no, no. I didn't mean that. Firm! Unalterable! Resolute! Ironwilled! Stonewall Jackson. That's the idea, isn't it?

BRASSBOUND (*hopelessly*). You are laughing at me.

LADY CECILY. No. Trembling, I assure you. Now will you try this on for me? I'm so afraid I have made it too tight under the arm. (*She holds it behind him.*)

BRASSBOUND (*obeying mechanically*). You take me for a fool, I think. (*He misses sleeve.*)

LADY CECILY. No; all men look foolish when they are feeling for their sleeves—

BRASSBOUND. Agh! (*He turns and snatches the coat from her; then puts it on himself and buttons the lowest button.*)

LADY CECILY (*horrified*). Stop. No, you must never pull a coat at the skirts, Captain Brassbound; it spoils the sit of it. Allow me. (*She pulls the lapels of his coat vigorously forward.*) Put back your shoulders. (*He frowns but obeys.*) That's better. (*She buttons the top button.*) Now button the rest, from the top down. Does it catch you at all under the arm?

BRASSBOUND (*miserably—all resistance beaten out of him*). No.

LADY CECILY. That's right. Now, before I go back to poor Marzo, say thank you to me for mending your jacket, like a nice polite sailor.

BRASSBOUND (*sitting down at the table in great agitation*). Damn you! You have belittled my whole life to me. (*He bows his head on his hands, convulsed.*)

LADY CECILY (*quite understanding, and putting her hand kindly on his shoulder*). Oh no. I am sure you have done lots of kind things and brave things, if you could only recollect them. With Gordon, for instance? Nobody can belittle that.

But the Sidi is on his way, and Captain Brassbound cannot now prevent his vengeance working itself out. However, an American gun-boat has been warned to keep an eye on the fate of the travellers, and by firing a few guns they succeed in frightening off the fanatics, and Captain Brassbound and his crew are marched off in custody.

The last act is delightful; in it the Captain, dressed by Lady Cecily's orders in her brother's, the Italian ambassador's, top hat and frock coat, looking appallingly stiff and grotesquely smart, comes up for court-martial with his crew. Lady Cecily explains everything away; how the two quarrelled when they found they were related, how well Captain Brassbound behaved; in short, she garbles the events in the most exquisitely ingenious fashion. Of course they are all acquitted. The play ends with Brassbound asking Lady Cecily what he is to do now, since she has knocked the bottom out of his old life. He blurts out a proposal of marriage, and she is almost hypnotized into saying yes; but the signal-gun breaks the spell, and he returns to his ship, glad that he has not persuaded her to sacrifice herself, and confident that he knows what is the secret of influence over men at last—disinterested, fearless sympathy.

The rare merit of the play lies in making you think most seriously of the relations of men to each other and laugh at the same time. Since Swift no such insistent preacher has so leavened his lesson with laughter. Dickens both preached and laughed, but he stopped laughing the moment he began to preach.

The humour in this play hovers perpetually on the edge of that tender emotion which the sight of great kindness and reasonableness stirs. Nowhere else, except in the second act of *Major Barbara,* is Mr. Shaw's emotional asceticism so perfectly justified by the results. This distrust of the melting mood is one of his most marked characteristics as a writer, and in a hortatory artist it is a sound instinct. For although men in a softened mood may take a deep impression more easily, such an impression is not likely to recur to them so often afterwards as those received at other times. The reformer does well, in conveying his moral, to aim at creating a mood which is more like those in which men ordinarily make their decisions. One reason why exciting harangues, whether moral or religious or political, influence so little the conduct of men who have nevertheless been deeply moved by them, is that the mood in which they felt the significance of what was said is one which normal circumstances rarely arouse again; the orator has "taken them out of themselves"; but the truths perceived when "they were themselves" are never quite forgotten.

The Court Theatre performance was below the usual mark, and not so good as that which the Stage Society gave some years before. It lacked those qualities of proportion and completeness which they have attained in almost every other case. The cast did not pull the play well together. Miss Ellen Terry contributed some delightful touches to the character of Lady Cecily, and all her own charm; but there was an absence of sureness in her acting sometimes, which spoilt its effect.

Mr. Frederick Kerr, as Brassbound, was not violent and dangerous enough. His attitudes and voice suggested an underlying fund of good nature, which detracts from the impressiveness of Lady Cecily's imperturbable serenity and her conquest of him. His "grrr-s" were guttural enough; but not sufficiently ferocious. It is important that he should behave with great brutality to her in the second act; so that completeness of the reaction of compunction, when he is overcome by her sweetness and kind good sense, may seem more natural and moving. Mr. Gwenn as Drinkwater was clever; but far too exaggerated; especially when he begs that his penny shockers may be returned to him. Mr. Cremlin made Rankin into a completely live human being. It is extraordinary what reality and solidity he can give to a part, provided it is one which fits his personality. Marzo was played quite perfectly. Johnson was very good: Mr. Edmund Gurney has a genius for reproducing the stolid self-satisfaction of the working-man.

How He Lied to her Husband

How he Lied to her Husband is not important. It might be described as a knock-about satire, for farce it is not; and if this description conveys the idea of a somewhat heart-damping entertainment, the impression is correct.

The acting of Miss Gertrude Kingston (She), Mr. Granville Barker (He), and Mr. Poulton (Bompas) was exceptionally good. The knocking-about was not very convincing; but that was inevitable, coming as it did in the middle of careful realistic acting. The characters are as contemptible as they are ridiculous, and yet real enough to make you believe in them. The result is you are on the whole more disgusted than amused; the story is too mean to yield anything but a seedy kind of fun. There are people who consider Maupassant's *L'Héritage* a good comic story; these may have found *How he Lied to her Husband* a light-hearted farce.

The Man of Destiny

This play was disappointing. The psychology appeared machine-made and obvious compared with Mr. Shaw's maturer work. Bonaparte is compounded and put together here after the Shavian prescription of a great man of action; the ingredients are nervous energy, unscrupulous determination, vanity well under control of the will, histrionic power, above all indifference towards happiness and a reckless disregard for personal dignity and honour, except when something can be gained from them by using them dramatically. The scene is laid in an Italian inn; the time is soon after the battle of Lodi. Some dispatches which Bonaparte expects have been wheedled out of the young blockhead of an aide-de-camp, by a lady disguised as an Austrian officer. The object of this confidence trick on her part was to prevent a private letter revealing some scandal about Josephine reaching the general.

The lady, after getting possession of the budget, puts up accidentally at the inn where Bonaparte is staying. He soon finds out that the young officer described by his lieutenant and the lady are the same person; and the rest of the play is a struggle for the letters. She is willing to hand them all over except one; he will not hear of this. Finally, he bullies her into yielding them all up; after which he reads the letter in question on the sly, and gives it back intact, as though he had been too magnanimous to read it; for he wishes to ignore the scandal, and the only dignified way of doing so is to pretend he knows nothing. When she discovers this, she is overcome with admiration for the courage which dares to do a mean thing, when it suits so perfectly his purpose. The fatuous young lieutenant is under arrest for having lost the dispatches and threatened with expulsion from the army unless he catches the Austrian who deceived him, which Bonaparte knows is impossible. The lady, however, outwits him by dressing up again as an Austrian officer and delivering herself up. At the end General Bonaparte and she are left alone together.

BONAPARTE (*throwing down the letters in a heap on the table*). Now! (*He sits down at the table in a chair he has placed*).

LADY. Yes; but you know you have *the* letter in your pocket. (*He smiles; takes a letter from his pocket, and tosses it on top of the heap. She holds it up and looks at him saying*) About Cæsar's wife.

BONAPARTE. Cæsar's wife is above suspicion. Burn it.

LADY (*taking up the snuffers and holding the letter to the candle flame with it*). I wonder would Cæsar's wife be above suspicion if she saw us here together!

BONAPARTE (*echoing her, with his elbows on the table and his cheeks on his hands, looking at the letter*). I wonder!

Miss Irene Vanbrugh's performance was graceful and spirited. Mr. Dion Boucicault as Bonaparte exaggerated his nervous restlessness. He represented him as merely a little demon of energy with fire-flashes of fury and impatience. But it was not only his fault that so little of Napoleon was represented; Mr. Shaw himself has not suggested Napoleon's impassive stolidity or his power of investing his *laissez-aller* moods with the air of profound purpose. One feels that Napoleon would have got those letters without making such a to-do about it.

THE DOCTOR'S DILEMMA

This is not among the best plays. It is a somewhat complicated story, which is made the vehicle of a great deal of hilarious, delightful satire on doctors and of some poor criticism upon the artistic temperament and the place of the artist in society. The story on the face of it looks quite simple: Sir Colenso Ridgeon, the discoverer of an antitoxin remedy for consumption, finds himself with only one vacancy in his sanatorium and two patients. His choice implies a death sentence upon one of them, since the treatment requires his personal supervision—indeed, it is a most dangerous one in other hands. The two sick men are an East End doctor, who is a commonplace honourable man, and a good-for-nothing artist with a real talent. Which life ought he to save? His dilemma is, however, complicated by his having taken a great fancy to the artist's wife. He knows this ought not to influence his decision; nor does it do so directly. But he finds that the wife has no conception that her husband is a worthless fellow; though, it is true, his ways have often landed them both in quandaries which were painful enough. Sooner or later, however, she is bound to find him out—and then what a tragedy for her! This consideration does, apparently, go some way towards deciding the issue in his mind against the artist. I say, apparently, because Ridgeon's motives are not made perfectly clear. This is a defect in the play.

In this dilemma his friend, old Sir Patrick Cullen, is his principal adviser. Sir Patrick is an old-fashioned doctor, a crusty and satisfying character, whose speech is shrewd and kindly, in whom moral work has become at last a kind of intellectual power—a metamorphosis we all have come across in life. When Sir Colenso Ridgeon confesses that his dilemma is complicated by his desire to marry Jennifer Dubedat, in the event of her husband's death, Sir Patrick tells him clearly that he must put that thought out of his mind in deciding; that it is a plain case of good picture or good man. And when Ridgeon, still half hankering after Jennifer, yet half genuinely in doubt, hesitates a preference for good art over good men, Sir Patrick says: "Don't talk your clever rubbish to me." Then with solemnity: "If you live in an age which turns to pictures, plays, and brass bands, because it can find nothing in humanity to ease its poor aching heart, then you may be thankful that you belong to a *noble* and *great* profession, whose business it is to heal men and women." Once more, after Dubedat is condemned to death, when Ridgeon explains that the principal consideration which determined him to cure Blenkinsop was that Jennifer might never suffer disillusionment, Sir Patrick's comment blows to shreds with one puff of caustic sense this phantasmal piece of casuistry: "It is rather hard on a young man to kill him simply because his wife has too high an opinion of him—fortunately many of us are not in that position." Ridgeon has made the right decision, but on the wrong grounds. Certainly this old Nestor of the profession has the *beau role*. Mr. William Farren, jun., played him in a way to make one feel, afterwards, that Sir Patrick Cullen must be some one one has known.

The first act takes place in Ridgeon's consulting-room, where five doctors call on him in succession to congratulate him on his knighthood, just conferred. While they are all talking about remedies and discoveries a woman is waiting to see him, and from time to time sends up an urgent request for an interview. Mrs. Dubedat refuses to be put off, and at last, through the entreaties of his old housekeeper, he consents to see her. She is told that her husband cannot be taken in as a patient, since the sanatorium is full. But when she shows some of her husband's drawings, their astonishing merit induces Ridgeon to make every effort to admit him, especially as he likes extremely Jennifer Dubedat herself. He asks her to bring her husband to a dinner at Richmond, where she will meet several eminent men of the profession, and they can all discuss the case together.

In Act II, the curtain discovers the five doctors, their host and Mrs. Dubedat sitting over coffee and cigarettes: Dubedat has just gone out to put on his coat, preparatory to an early start home. They have all been charmed with the young artist and his wife, except Sir Patrick, who has his suspicions. You cannot tell, he says, what a man is, until you know his behaviour with regard to money and women. Dubedat returns for a few minutes to fetch Jennifer, and they go off with Ridgeon's emphatic promise that he will undertake the cure. Alone together, the five men begin discussing the artist, and it comes out that he has tried to borrow money from three of them, successfully in two cases; and they have hardly got over their dismay, when one of the maids comes in to ask for the address of the gentleman who has just gone away "with that woman": she turns out to be Dubedat's lawful wife. In addition to these damaging discoveries, poor Blenkinsop enters, terribly upset at having failed to catch Dubedat before he started, because he has borrowed his last half-crown. Before the evening is out he confesses, somewhat reluctantly, to his friends that his own lungs also are touched. Ridgeon decides, after talking over the matter, to save Blenkinsop, and Dubedat is handed over to the mercies of Sir Ralph Bloomfield Bonington.

Act III. Sir Ralph, Sir Patrick, Cutler Walpole, and Ridgeon visit Dubedat's studio to confront him with his misdeeds and to explain to his wife that Sir Ralph will undertake the case instead. Dubedat meets their indignation with dumbfounding placidity. He has no conscience whatever about anything outside his work; but as far as that is concerned he allows nothing to prevent him from doing his best. In this scene he actually tries to borrow money from Ridgeon, on the security of a post-dated cheque, which will enable Ridgeon to blackmail Jennifer into paying him more than he lends.

The last act, in which Dubedat dies in front of the footlights, has been the subject of a good deal of discussion. Mr. Granville Barker acted the death naturally and realistically. Fault was found with him on the ground that a death struggle untouched by artistic emotion is an unfair, unilluminating assault on the emotions. But it was necessary that we should realize that chilly, quiet, matter-of-factness of physical extinction, so terribly inconsistent with all we know death means, at the very moment of feeling pity for a man whose will is still ablaze, and whose mind is clear and detached in spite of the creeping languor of death. For Dubedat dies in a pose. He hoards his last strength and his last words to stamp an image of himself on his wife's heart which he knows is not the true one. Next to his immortality in his pictures, he values that reincarnation most. He keeps an interviewer in the room, in the hope that some faint reflection of himself, as he would wish to be remembered, may possibly be thrown also upon the great blank sheet of the public imagination. The cheerful and callous young ass of an interviewer conveys by a few words, after all is over, that he has taken away a grotesquely topsy-turvy idea, such as would have disgusted the dead man and made him laugh sourly enough. That is a telling piece of irony; but profounder still is the irony of the success of Dubedat's pose upon his wife; nothing can henceforth shake her conviction that he is a hero, a king of men. She turns to the doctors, who have let him die because they judged him unworthy, and appeals to them as though they were all standing together on the top of a mountain of transfiguration. In this last scene Dubedat obeyed the same instinct which drove him in life to create beautiful pictures. His last picture is painted on his wife's mind. This is the climax of the play; it is followed by an anticlimax which completes the story.

Ridgeon and Jennifer meet at an exhibition of Dubedat's pictures. She challenges him with being indirectly responsible for her husband's death. "Confess to a failure and save our friendship." He admits straight out that he killed Dubedat. But she does not understand at first what he means by this admission. It only gradually dawns on her that he left her husband to die on purpose, and that his motive was a desire to marry her himself, and to shield her from the discovery that her husband was an unmitigated rascal. She is amazed at the idea that he should have been in love with her all the time, and still more at his dreaming she could care for him in return.

"You—an elderly man!" At this reply he staggers back and cries, "O Dubedat, thou art avenged!" A moment later he hears that, in obedience to her late husband's wish, she has married again, and the play ends with this last exclamation, "Then I have committed a completely disinterested murder."

This epilogue is disastrous. Firstly, it tends to trivialize the impression the play has made; for though the last line in it may be, in intention, a summing up of the irony of the story, it rings out fatally in the key of burlesque, like the previous exclamation. Secondly, Ridgeon does not do justice to his own motives; he did not decide against Dubedat entirely because he coveted his wife, or because he wished to save her from disillusionment; so this admission on his part confuses the audience's recollection of what has gone before.

Now to return to the characters and the acting. Sir Ralph Bloomfield Bonington (fashionable physician) is a masterpiece. A critic in search of emphasis may choose between saying that the part was worthy of Mr. Eric Lewis's acting, or that Mr. Eric Lewis's acting was worthy of the part; either statement implies absolute praise. Long will "B. B.," the frockcoated, rosy-gilled babbler of scientific jargon and impromptu consolations, hang in our imaginations! Mr. Lewis's optimistic, confident tenor voice and Micawber-like alacrity of gesture, his air of sympathetic concern, his soothing courtesy of assent as he hovered over his patient or listened to the anxieties of the wife, were perfect. He is at once typical and individual, and, therefore, not simply a caricature. Cutler Walpole (Mr. James Hearn) is a caricature of the brusque, hard-headed type of surgeon, whose manner seems to say, "Pooh, man! the body has no mysteries for us now. Trust me, I'll put that right in a jiffy." "B. B." inspires confidence and holds together a fashionable practice by blandishment and his own natural buoyancy, Cutler Walpole by bluff; both succeed completely in taking in themselves as well. Mr. Michael Sherbrooke as the little German Jew doctor, who had scraped together a nice little fortune by using the magic words "cure guaranteed," was complete, from the gleam of his spectacles to the rasp of his accent. The poor but honest Blenkinsop is almost too worthy an individual to engage real sympathy. After Dubedat as gone off with his last half-crown on the night of the dinner at Richmond, he actually refuses the loan of an Underground fare from Ridgeon, whom he has known for twenty years, for fear his friends should dread his borrowing money on other occasions. This is carrying rugged independence to the extent of becoming a social incubus, and one's sympathies begin to incline towards Dubedat. Mr. Gurney found a wonderfully expressive manner for Blenkinsop; a kind of deprecating, big-dog shyness which suggested a loyal, modest nature. Ridgeon was Mr. Webster's best part. In appearance he bore an odd resemblance to the Millais portrait of Ruskin. His slightly pompous, educated voice and his self-conscious gestures, both so habitually controlled that they can no longer betray emotion, only express it intentionally, and the suggestions of intellectual refinement in his manner, were all traits of an admirably acted, real character.

Miss McCarthy as Jennifer conveyed the romance of her part. She was admirable when pleading for her husband's life in the first act.

Dubedat was played by Mr. Barker as well as the drawing of the character allowed. He suggested perfectly the character of a rather agreeably uppish, slouching, loose young blackguard at the dinner; and he died well. But the psychology of the character is far too crude to be convincing. The incidents intended to show him up occur with an artificial appositeness, and Dubedat himself is mechanically constructed on the old unsatisfactory formula of "the artistic temperament," that dismal relic of the art for art's sake movement, so wretchedly barren itself in England.

The avoidance of all artificial appositeness, unreality, or improbability is absolutely essential to the impressiveness of a Shavian play, and the presence of such blemishes is particularly deadly to them for this reason: Mr. Shaw's aim as a dramatist is to correct our conception of the normal, which has been disturbed by a conventional treatment of human nature on the stage. His characters and situations consequently strike the playgoer at first as strange and fantastic; it is with difficulty that he can believe them real; they are so different from what he expected to see. If, therefore, the action and situations deviate in the slightest degree from probability, the whole play, characters and all, in which the ludicrous and astonishing are already so strangely mingled, takes on the air of a fantastic and arbitrary creation. Only the man whose matter-of-factness is above suspicion can convince us that something unexpected is true; and Mr. Shaw deals almost entirely with the unexpected. The points at which he has deviated from matter-of-fact plausibility in this play are Dubedat's conduct in the studio and on the night of the dinner; Jennifer's behaviour in the epilogue; and the simultaneous morning visits, of the four doctors with leading practices, on two separate occasions, to the studio of an impoverished artist, where only one had professional business. "Now," says the spectator to himself, "the man who will bend facts like this, may well give human nature a twist: I believe this is a clever puppet-show." He is quite wrong, but the mistake is excusable.

THE PHILANDERER

This is a queer piece of work, and finds its place very properly among the "Unpleasant" plays. It was not very successful at the Court for the reason that to make the play intelligible, Charteris must be acted by some one who understands him perfectly, and such a person probably does not exist. Just as in the playing of Dubedat it is absolutely necessary that the actor should bring out something in his character, to explain why his victims never sent for the police (which Mr. Barker succeeded in doing), so the actor who takes the part of Charteris must make it clear why he is not periodically kicked. He was exasperating and he was disliked, but he was not that sort of person. This can only be conveyed through something in his manner and in his way of saying things. Mr. Webster in the part certainly did not appear like a man who gets kicked; but it was his own dignity and his own personality, not Charteris's, that were apparent.

Charteris is a very exceptional character. I hazard as an explanation of his immunity and his influence on others, not his wit or cleverness, but the impression he made of being a fantastically honest man; people instinctively felt that he had administered to himself so many moral kickings as to make any they could add an unnecessary impertinence. In one of his talks with the discarded Julia, he says, "I confess I am either something more or something less than a gentleman; you used to give me the benefit of the doubt." It is possible, however, to be both at the same time, and that is precisely what he was. Charteris's honesty in his philanderings was morally superior to the code of the conventional gentleman in such matters, which is to continue to simulate respect for the self-respect of the woman, when he knows it to be a sham in which she does not believe herself, in order that she may return the compliment; but on the other hand he fell far below the gentleman in the wanton cruelty with which he used his cleverness to hurt his victims without their being able to understand what he meant. He was not a coxcomb physically or morally, his vanity was superficial; but intellectually he was a cruel coxcomb. For instance, in one of his last interviews with Julia, he exclaims, "Oh, what I have learnt from you!—from *you* who could learn nothing from me! I made a fool of you, and you brought me wisdom; I broke your heart, and you brought me joy; I made you curse your womanhood, and you revealed my manhood to me. Blessings, for ever and ever, on my Julia's name!" (with genuine emotion, he takes her hand and kisses it). Julia, who does not understand, snatches away her hand, saying, "Oh, stop talking that nasty sneering stuff." Where Charteris behaves like a cad, is in not leaving her alone after he has disentagled himself, but in continuing to vivisect her when he knows she can learn nothing from these painful experiments. His general philandering he justified on the ground that it was always instructive to both parties; here he had no such excuse.

Again, the match between Dr. Paramore and Julia, which is so much against her natural inclination, is engineered by Charteris to free himself from her persecutions; and there is something so cruel in his using his cleverness and his knowledge of "the very pulse of the machine" to contrive it, that the spectator is disgusted.

The play, like all artistic work which has aimed in its day at being up-to-date, strikes us now as old-fashioned. It is a product of the early eighteen-nineties, when Ibsen first arrived as a moral prophet on our shores and people went about trying to "realize themselves"; when the moral of *The Doll's House* was taken as the solution of marriage and sex difficulties; when women were very conscious of being emancipated and determined to sink the "he and she" in all relations and to "belong to themselves"; in fact of the period when *The Heavenly Twins* and *The Woman Who Did,* and similar books appeared.

Mr. Shaw sympathized with the woman's movement, as his *Quintessence of Ibsenism* remains to show; but as a critical observer he saw clearly enough that many women who went in for emancipating themselves had not thrown off the "old" woman when they put on the "new." This play is a satire which exposes such women effectively enough. However, the "new woman" no longer exists, nor do such old-fashioned fathers as Cuthbertson and Craven who talk about "manly men and womanly women"; so the satire directed against them does not seem now to hit a mark worth aiming at.

The kind of comedy extracted from the situations which expose the wretched Julia, is not the kind to make one laugh. A man in the clutches of a jealous termagant might chuckle with delight to see Julia stripped and whipped; but, really, some kind of interested animus is necessary to appreciate this kind of fun; though there are witty things throughout the dialogue which everybody can enjoy, such as this passage for instance.

CHARTERIS. I accuse you of stealing letters of mine.
JULIA (*rising*). Yes, nice letters!
CHARTERIS.—Of breaking your solemn promises not to do it again; of spending hours—aye, days!—piecing together the contents of my wastepaper basket in your search for more letters. . . .
JULIA. I was justified in reading your letters. Our perfect confidence in one another gave me the right to do it.

Miss Wynne-Matthison played Grace Tranfield, who refuses to marry the Philanderer, with perfect accuracy. The most delightfully-acted character in the piece was Cuthbertson (Mr. Luigi Lablache).

MAJOR BARBARA

I have not considered *Major Barbara* in its chronological place, because it and *Don Juan in Hell* lead naturally to the remarks upon Mr. Shaw's philosophy, with which it will be well to end these criticisms of his plays. *Major Barbara* is the story of a woman who lives in her religion and loses it; who, after enduring the desolation of seeing her own and all the world's hope hang torn before her eyes, finds at last a belief her passionate heart can live by. This account will seem ridiculous to those who heard only the crackle of wit, the rhetoric of theory, and brisk interchange of comment; yet it is the centre and significance of the play.

It is the first English play which has for its theme the struggle between two religions in one mind. And to have written upon that theme convincingly is a triumph, which criticism cannot appreciably lessen. The second act is "wonderful, most wonderful, and yet again wonderful, and after that past all whooping."

Barbara is the daughter of the chief partner in the biggest cannon-manufactory in the world. Her mother is a lady of birth and position, "well mannered yet appallingly outspoken and indifferent to the opinions of her interlocutors, arbitrary and high-tempered to the last bearable degree, full of class prejudices, conceiving the universe exactly as if it were a large house in Wilton Crescent, though handling her corner of it very effectively on that assumption." Barbara's parents have been living apart for years.

When the play begins, the engagement of Lady Britomart's two daughters to young men without money has compelled her to ask her husband to call upon her in order that she may persuade him to make a fitting provision for them. The one daughter is a very ordinary society girl; the other, Barbara, has a genius for saving souls, and is already a prominent officer in the Salvation Army. She is engaged to Cusins, a professor of Greek, who fell in love with her and proposed under the impression that she was an ordinary Salvation Army lass.

The first act introduces these people, and its interest lies in the return of Undershaft to the bosom of his family. Lady Britomart was admirably played by Miss Filippi. On Undershaft's being announced I had a vivid recollection of her adjusting her spectacles and settling herself in a chair facing the door with an admirable air of nervous decision. Mr. Calvert's Undershaft was not nearly so good as his blusterous Broadbent or his balmy "William"; for Undershaft was good-natured and easy-going on the surface but fuliginous and formidable underneath, but Mr. Calvert was complacent underneath and formidable on the surface. Of all Undershaft's family Barbara alone interests him, and his heart goes out to her, though he would resent such a description of his feelings. They both have religious natures, but the beliefs of each are poles asunder. Each wishes to convert the other, and they strike a bargain; he will visit her Salvation Army shelter, if she will afterwards visit his gun-manufactory. The second act is laid at the shelter.

There is no space in which to dilate upon the pathos, passion, and significant realism of this scene, or upon the ironic ectasy which Cusins contributes to it (imagine the difficulty of acting such a purely intellectual passion!) but one incident must be noted. Bill Walker, a bullying sort of ruffian, slouches in to recover "his girl," who has been recently converted; and when one of the Salvation lasses tells him she has gone away, he hits her in the mouth. Now, this blow very nearly brings about his own conversion; for Jenny Hill does not resent it, and Major Barbara takes advantage of the shame which begins to stir in him to make him more and more uncomfortable. His impulse is to buy back his peace of mind and self-respect by getting thrashed by his girl's new Salvation Army "bloke," and failing in this, he offers Jenny a sovereign. Barbara tells him he cannot buy his salvation; she wants to touch his heart, and if he were to think he had made amends, he would go away as stupid and brutal as he came. Her father all the while watches this soul-saving process with grim sympathy. His chance comes when the news arrives that Bodger, the whisky-distiller, has offered a £5,000 subscription if another £5,000 can be raised. The money is of vital importance to the Army; indeed this shelter will have to be closed if funds are not forthcoming. Barbara has already refused £100 from her father for the same reason that she refused Bill's twenty shillings—because she wants her father to give up manufacturing the means of death; and if he can ease his conscience by being charitable, he will go on making money out of the sufferings of men. But the Army does not attach so much importance to the saving of Undershaft's soul, as to the power his money will give them to help many others; so when he offers to make up the other £5,000 they accept it with grateful thanksgivings and Hallelujahs. This is a terrible shock to Barbara, who realizes, for the first time, that the power of the Army rests ultimately on the support of its worst enemies; who make the money they give away out of the very misery and degradation which the Army fights. The other side to this view is put by Mrs. Baines: "Who would have thought that any good could have come out of war and drink? And yet their profits are brought to-day to the feet of salvation to do its blessed work." Barbara sees that Bodger "wants to send his cheque down to buy us and go on being as wicked as ever"; while Cusins exclaims with excited irony, "The millennium will be inaugurated by the unselfishness of Undershaft and Bodger. O be joyful!" The Army must accept the money, since they are powerless without it; but the fact that they are right to accept it, shows that they are fighting a battle they can never win; since if once they begin to make real headway against Bodger, his subscriptions, which are their means of victory, will be cut off. Barbara realizes this on reflection; but at the moment it is the revelation of the spring whence the Army's power is drawn, coupled with the object lesson that the Army cannot afford to think of the individual soul while such supplies are in question, which tumbles her faith to the ground. She is quite certain that a crusade which draws its strength from the evils it wishes to destroy, cannot put the world straight. This is a criticism which hits all the Churches and all Charitable Institutions in so far as they hope to do this. From a revolutionist's point of view, they are also objectionable, because they tend to keep the poor quiet, by making them less discontented with conditions which they ought to die rather than stand, and the rich from thinking they are just and honest, by offering them opportunities of being generous and kind; in short, because they keep those who should be indignant, servile, and those who ought to be uneasy, self-satisfied.

Undershaft's gospel, on its social side, is to preach socialism to the rich and rebellion to the poor, whereby he twists the same rope from both ends. The most important fact to insist upon is, therefore, the importance of money; tacitly, this is recognized by every one; the possession of comfortable independence being everywhere the most universally powerful motive. But instead of blinking this fact and preaching "Blessed are the poor," while taking care at the same time to have a reliable source of income ourselves, we must preach "Cursed be the poor," so that every poverty-stricken man may either feel he has a grievance not to be borne, or be ashamed of the feebleness which keeps him so. The way in which Undershaft puts it is that poverty is literally *the worst of crimes*, and it follows from this assertion that a man is right to commit any other crime to avoid that one, should circumstances force him into such a dilemma. Now this is a doctrine that good sense refuses to swallow. How then did Undershaft or Mr. Shaw come to believe it, and urge it with such vehemence?

The temperament and interests of a reformer drive him to look continually at results of actions and emotions in valuing them rather than at these things themselves; and since poverty and ill-health are probably the causes of more evil than is any single vice, the reformer slips more readily than other people into the mistake of thinking that these things are, in themselves, worse than any vice. But it is clear that what may be a cause of evil is often not even bad at all in itself, let alone not so bad as the evil; and equally, that the means to good are often valueless in themselves, compared to what they help to bring about. That poverty is not bad in itself—is no more a crime than is a broken leg—is so clear that if a man of Mr. Shaw's talents had not said it was, no critic would bore his reader with a refutation of such a statement. Bunyan and Blake, whom Mr. Shaw praises with such liberality of genuine admiration, were very poor; yet that they were among the most ignoble of criminals he himself would never admit.

It is clear that poverty, like ill-health, is only bad as a difficulty in the way of a fine life which a few surmount, and that therefore the pretext of escaping from it cannot justify the worst actions. Indeed, if Undershaft's doctrine were generally believed, the only effect would be to make poverty the cause of much more evil, of many more acts of violence, oppression and meanness, than it is now. Dubedat took every means in his power—blackmailing, stealing, utilizing his wife's charms as bait—to escape poverty; yet I do not think Undershaft would have felt that he was doing much to bring about a better state of things.

And Undershaft himself? He talks very big about having been prepared to kill anybody as long as he was poor; but what did he *do*? Did he found his fortunes by knocking an old woman on the head and stealing her watch, or by going into partnership with a Mrs. Warren? No, of course not; he stuck to his desk like a good young man, inched and pinched until he had made himself useful to the firm, and then took good care not to be put upon. Undershaft's weakness lay in talking big; that is really what his sensible wife could not stand. In Act II he tells his son that he and Lazarus are really the people who govern England, and decide questions of war and peace; and in Act III he explains to Cusins that he is a fool if he accepts the partnership in the hope of power, since he and Lazarus are in fact absolutely powerless. In both cases he is talking big.

In this third and last act Barbara and her family visit the town of Perivale St. Andrews. They find it is a clean, fine place, where everybody is well-fed and well-clad. It is, in fact, a kind of socialistic community with this great difference; instead of being pervaded with a spirit of equality and independence, the whole place is honey-combed with snobbishness and petty oppression. This spirit is what

Barbara will spend her life now in fighting. Her work will be amongst uppish, vulgar, prosperous self-satisfied people, and her last speech is a pæan of rejoicing that she will in future never feel the humiliation of knowing that the truths she has at heart are listened to because she distributes alms at the same time.

The last act is weak on the stage; indeed the defect of the play is that Barbara's conversion is much less impressive than the loss of her old religion. Miss Annie Russell, who was so good in the first two acts, could make little of the third.

The moral of the play filtered from Undershaft's plutocratic gospel would run as follows: that the ideal state is one in which no one is poor; that the ideal man is he who shifts vigorously for himself; that the best cure for the present anarchic and miserable state of things, is that every individual should become self-reliant and use the weapons which Undershaft manufactures against those who oppress him; that those who have already some wealth and independence are the people it is most profitable to teach what is good; that to the rest it is more important to preach rebellion. If *Man and Superman* is in a sense the cry of a reformer clinging to the idea of selective breeding of mankind as the last hen-coop in the wreck of his hopes, *Major Barbara* expresses the disappointed impatience of a pamphleteer who gives up his belief in persuasion and turns to the swifter agency of force. The fallacy which the play attacks with perfect justice, is that of preaching to or of helping the poor simply because they are *poor*.

DON JUAN IN HELL

The mistake into which Mr. Shaw slips of saying that poverty is a crime far worse than murder or lust or avarice, since it is perhaps a more constant *cause* of crime and feebleness than any one of these, is a fallacy which in one form or other often occurs in his writings. His great defect as an artist-philosopher is that he does not distinguish between those things which are bad as means and those which are bad in themselves, or between what is good as an end and what is only good as a means to that end; that when he judges the actions and emotions or the lives and characters of men and women, his test is invariably—What use are they? If he feels them to be useful as a means to reforming society, then they are good; if they cannot be shown to be useful, or only to be less useful than something else, then they are judged to be comparatively valueless. But it is certain that qualities and things which are valuable as means are not necessarily worth having for their own sakes, and that things very good in themselves may not at the same time be important as means to something else worth having. And since this is indubitably true, it follows that any one who judges the values of things from the point of view of their results, and hardly ever asks himself whether they have any value in themselves, must often get his scale of values wrong. This is the most general criticism which can be brought against the morality of the Shavian drama. A great part of that originality of view which underlies the plays is due to the fact that he judges goodness and badness by their results alone. The transvaluation which follows is often startling; actions which nobody thought particularly bad are put in a class with the most heinous offences, and qualities not commonly allowed to be claims upon the respect of others are exalted above affection. In this he is often right, because the goodness of things as a means may be an important part of their total value; but he is, also, often wrong, because the importance of anything as a means to something else may be a very small part of its total value. For instance, what are the qualities most extolled in his plays? Vitality, pugnacity, political and intellectual honesty, fearlessness and universal benevolence: these are clearly useful. What are the qualities and emotions which on the whole are depreciated or pointedly ignored? Personal affections, admiration, and sensitiveness to beauty: these cannot be shown to be such powerful means towards bringing about a better state of society; but are they not essential elements in that better state itself? Mr. Shaw ignores the question of ultimate ends so completely that when he defines Heaven, the ideal state, he describes it as a community of men working towards bringing it into existence. "In Heaven you live and work, instead of playing and pretending, you face things as they are; you escape nothing but glamour, and your steadfastness and your peril are your glory. . . . But even as you [the devil] enjoy the contemplation of such romantic mirages as beauty and pleasure, so would I enjoy the contemplation of that which interests me about all things: namely, Life: the force that ever strives to attain greater power of contemplating itself." The point which I wish to insist upon here is not that Mr. Shaw is not right in considering his Heaven superior to his Hell—it obviously is; but that his Heaven is not the contemplation of what is perfect, but of something that is struggling to become so. It is a condition in which there is still peril, where you "face things as they are"; in short, a "community of saints" which is really a community of reformers. Mr. Shaw describes them as filled with "a passion of the divine will"; but this passion is a desire to make the world better, and not a contemplation of perfection: in so far as it is a contemplative ecstasy at all, it is only rapture at the idea that perfection is possible. What chills us, then, in his Heaven is the misgiving that the phrase "masters of reality" (so the heavenly inhabitants are described) is a euphemism for a society of people all devoted to making each other and everybody else more virtuous. Now we can imagine something better than that; and Mr. Shaw's Hell, if he had not been so grossly unfair to it, seems to offer a better foundation for its construction. Hell is a community in which personal relations and the contemplation of beauty are the supreme goods. Mr. Shaw cheapens this ideal by assuming that the only kind of love which can compete with the fellow-service of heaven is a kind which might be worthily sung by Sedley, or set to music by Offenbach, or depicted by Fragonard. No one requires to be told that Mohammed's paradise, however intellectualized and refined, is not the highest good; but what is instructive in Mr. Shaw's antithesis is that he sets so much store by the contemplation of what is both real and beautiful at the same time, raising this above the contemplation of beauty or goodness which is not accompanied by a true belief in the object. That this judgment is a true one nobody can doubt; what can be protested against with equal justice is the assumption that love between individuals always implies contemplation of goodness and beauty which cannot be believed to be real.

The performance of *Don Juan in Hell* could only have been very interesting to those who enjoy an abstract discussion; but as a spectacle it must have delighted all. The dresses, designed by Mr. Charles Ricketts, were most beautiful; Mr. Robert Loraine's performance was a triumph of memory, if not of elocution. Mr. Michael Sherbrooke, as the Statue, declared his sentiments in an admirably military voice. Miss McCarthy was particularly good as the old woman, and radiant in her transformation.

The analysis of these eleven plays has not been elaborate enough to require a summary; but there are a few points which may be added in conclusion.

As a dramatist Mr. Shaw's gift for caricature is a perpetual temptation to him, leading him often to destroy the atmosphere of reality which is so important to his plays. Though his caricatures are good in themselves, he has not always sufficient artistic self-control to keep them in their places. Moreover, that emotional asceticism, which has been already commented upon, is always tempting him to create in the spectator the balance of mind and emotion he respects by alternately touching him and making him laugh. This method succeeds when the scene, rousing a mixed emotion of sympathy and contempt, is a crude one, such as Broadbent's courting and comforting of Nora Reilly in *John Bull's Other Island*. But frequently this cannot be done by a series of consequent shocks; for the emotion which ought to be roused by Mr. Shaw's situations is often too complex and delicate to be produced by such galvanic methods. Sir Ralph's harangue after the death of Dubedat is an instance of its failure.

One character in *The Doctor's Dilemma* remarks, "Life does not cease to be funny when people die any more than it ceases to be serious when people laugh," which would be a good motto for most of Mr. Shaw's plays. But what he constantly overlooks, as an artist, is that for a man who is feeling its tragedy, life does for the time cease to be comic. He relies, then, as an artist, too much on an exceptional flexibility of emotion in his audience. His weakness as a philosopher is to judge the value of human beings and emotions too exclusively by their usefulness towards furthering another end; as a propagandist, to under-rate the intelligence of the average man.

His merits—if my criticisms have not suggested that these are remarkable, I have utterly failed. He has drawn more characters which are immediately recognized and understood than any other English dramatist with the exception of Shakespeare; he has chosen for his subjects situations which are really interesting; and he has made us laugh and think at the same time.

Every author of any power has a peculiar contagion. The contagion that we catch from Mr. Shaw's plays is an admiration for courage and intellectual honesty, and for a kind of spontaneity of character which is a blending of both. His plays attack hypocrisy by showing that men have more reason to be ashamed of the disguises of their egotism, than of their egotism itself. The influence of his writings tends to make them found their self-respect rather on their indubitable qualities than on their aspirations, and to prevent them looking for more in life and human nature than they are likely to find. The intention of the greater part of his work is to provide an antidote to romantic despair by forestalling disillusionment, and to stimulate an active and gay resolution in the place of an exasperated seclusion of spirit or indifference, either gloomy or light. Its danger for some is to breed in them such pride of courage in facing the triviality and ugliness of life, that they come to hate an ideal which may be better than reality, simply because it is not a fact. Mr. Shaw often warns us against calling his golden grapes of riches sour, but he has not warned us against disparaging celestial fruits, because they are out of our reach. He has still to write his *Wild Duck*, which I take it will be a satire on "The Shavians," who derive a perverted gratification from the flatness of life and from the stupendous extent of the social improvements necessary, on account of the scope these offer for the exercise of a light-hearted courage in "facing facts" and for triumphing over more sensitive natures. All his work is marked by a straightforward dexterity of execution, which is in itself an æsthetic merit; and almost every play he has written stimulates that social consciousness of communal responsibility upon which the hopes of reformers depend.

CONCLUSION

At the close of such a commentary as this, in which many plays and many actors have been reviewed, it is natural to wonder somewhat anxiously what general impression may have been left behind; to what extent exceptious observations may have seemed to detract unduly from achievement, or how heavily expressions of admiration, owing to a general depreciation in the currency of praise, may have been discounted in the reader's mind. In consequence of such misgivings critics are apt in their conclusions to relax the stringency of their standards, and to fall into a strain of almost obituary benevolence. When the subject of the criticism is some author who has said his best, or some movement which has done its work, such leniency is fitting enough; but here, in the case of this enterprise, which has just finished the first period of its career in triumph, and is starting on the next with public gratitude and enthusiasm behind it, such a tone would be absurdly inappropriate. It requires no coddling at the hands of critics. I have not the least fear that, among those who saw many of these plays, the record of any blemishes will impair the favourable impressions they received; but in the case of those who saw none or only a few, it is necessary to guard against possible misunderstanding, should they ever read these pages.

It is common to complain of the censoriousness of gossip, and to attribute the severity of such comments as pass behind people's backs to ill-nature, when they were really due to the fact that the most *interesting* truths about a particular person happened to be concerned with his faults. In the same way, and for the same reason, the critic finds himself dwelling upon defects; they may be even the defects of good qualities—a needle cannot be sharp at both ends—but if they are more interesting than the merits themselves he is bound to give them close attention. Moreover, from those who give much, much is expected. The reason why criticism is so liable to get out of proportion is that the presence of some real merit is necessary to rouse the critical faculty at all, with the result that such works as possess it do not get praised in the same wholehearted fashion as those which cannot provoke comparison with high achievement.

The work of the Vedrenne-Barker management has been remarkable enough to challenge the highest standards, and therefore to sharpen the eyes of critics. Certainly (if I may speak for myself) I should not have felt so keenly when anything was lacking in their performances had they not shown me at the same time to what pitch of excellence it is possible to attain.

APPENDIX I.

(Appendix to the Original Edition)

Reprinted Programmes of the Vedrenne-Barker
Performances at the Court Theatre

APPENDIX

THE following pages contain exact reprints of all programmes of the "Vedrenne-Barker" management,[1] except in a half-a-dozen instances when plays were revived with casts identical or almost identical with those of previous runs; such revivals and alterations are noted at the foot of the earlier programmes. The programmes are arranged in chronological order according to the date of the first performance of each run.

"The Vedrenne-Barker Performances," strictly speaking, began on October 18, 1904, and lasted at the Court Theatre until June 29, 1907. During that time 32 plays by 17 authors were produced, and 946 performances were given; but, since one triple-bill and four double-bills were included, the total number of performances of separate plays amounts to 988, distributed amongst authors as follows:—

Shaw (11 plays) . . .	701	Hauptmann	9
Houseman and Barker .	48	Schnitzler	9
Euripides (3 plays) . .	48	Yeats	9
Barker	34	C. Harcourt	8
Galsworthy	29	Masefield	8
Hankin (2 plays) . . .	27	Maeterlinck	6
Robins	23	R. V. Harcourt	2
Ibsen (2 plays) . . .	13	Fenn	2
Hewlett (2 plays) . .	12		988

[1]The first programme, of six matinées of *Candida* in April and May, 1904, is included as showing the beginning of these performances; but they are not regarded as belonging strictly to the "Vedrenne-Barker" series, and are not counted in the ensuing table, nor in the above figures.

PLAY.	AUTHOR.	PERFORMANCES.	PROGRAMMES ON PAGE
Man and Superman	Bernard Shaw	176	122, 127, 142,152
You Never Can Tell	,, ,,	149	120, 123, 138, 146
John Bull's Other Island . . .	,, ,,	121	111, 115, 119, 124, 139
Capt. Brassbound's Conversion .	,, ,,	89	135
Major Barbara	,, ,,	52	129, 130
The Doctor's Dilemma	,, ,,	50	143
Prunella	Housman and Barker	48	114, 137, 151
The Voysey Inheritance . . .	Granville Barker	34	128, 133
Candida	Bernard Shaw	31	113, 121
The Silver Box	J. Galsworthy	29	140, 148
Votes for Women	Elizabeth Robins	23	149
The Electra	Euripides	20	131
The Hippolytus	,,	20	110, 136
The Return of the Prodigal . .	St. John Hankin	19	125, 150
The Thieves' Comedy	G. Hauptmann	9	117
The Pot of Broth	W. B. Yeats	9	} (triple bill) 116
In the Hospital	A. Schnitzler	9	
How he Lied to her Husband .	Bernard Shaw	9	
The Trojan Women	Euripides	8	118
The Charity that began at Home	St. John Hankin	8	141
The Reformer	Cyril Harcourt	8	} (double bill) 144
The Campden Wonder	John Masefield	8	
The Philanderer	Bernard Shaw	8	145
Don Juan in Hell	,, ,,	8	} (double bill) 153
The Man of Destiny	,, ,,	8	
Hedda Gabler	Henrik Ibsen	7	147
Aglavaine and Selysette . . .	M. Materlinck	6	112
The Wild Duck	Henrik Ibsen	6	126
Pan and the Young Shepherd .	Maurice Hewlett	6	} (double bill) 134
The Youngest of the Angels . .	,, ,,	6	
A Question of Age	R. V. Harcourt	2	} (double bill) 132
The Convict on the Hearth . .	F. Fenn	2	
		988	

1904.

April 26th, 29th, May 3rd, 5th, 6th, and 10th.

CANDIDA

By Bernard Shaw.

Candida	Miss KATE RORKE
Proserpine Garnett	Miss SYDNEY FAIR-BROTHER
The Rev. James Mavor Morell	Mr. NORMAN McKINNEL
Eugene Marchbanks	Mr. GRANVILLE BARKER
Mr. Burgess	Mr. A. G. POULTON
The Rev. Alexander Mill ...	Mr. ATHOL STEWART

The Action takes place at St. Dominic's Vicarage, Victoria

Park, E.

An October Day, 1894.

ACT I. Morning.   ACT II. Afternoon.   ACT III. Evening.

NOTE.—These performances are not counted in the enumeration of the Vedrenne-Barker series.

1904.

On October 18th, 20th, 21st, 25th, 27th and
28th, at 3 p.m.,

THE HIPPOLYTUS OF EURIPIDES

Translated by Gilbert Murray.

The Goddess Aphrodite ...	Miss ELINOR FOSTER
The Goddess Artemis ...	Miss GWENDOLEN BISHOP
Theseus (*King of Athens and Trozên*)	Mr. ALFRED BRYDONE
Phaedra (*Daughter of Minos, King of Crete, Wife of Theseus*)	Miss EDYTH OLIVE
Hippolytus (*Bastard son of Theseus and the Amazon Hippolytê*)	Mr. BEN WEBSTER
Henchman	Mr. GRANVILLE BARKER
An Old Huntsman	Mr. A. E. GEORGE
The Nurse	Miss ROSINA FILIPPI
Leader of Chorus	Miss TITA BRAND

Chorus of Trozenean Women:

MISS FLORENCE FARR, MISS DOROTHY THOMAS,
MISS AMY LAMBORN, MISS MAY MARTYN,
MISS MAUD YATES, MISS INTHEA PITZ,
MISS INESCOURT, MISS FLORENCE STONE,
MISS DEROS, MISS SANDBERG,
MISS GERTRUDE AYLWARD, MISS WEIGALL.

1904.

On November 1st, 3rd, 4th, 8th, 10th, and 11th,
1904, at 2.30 p.m.,

JOHN BULL'S OTHER ISLAND

A New and Unpublished Play by Bernard Shaw.

Broadbent	Mr. LOUIS CALVERT
Larry Doyle	Mr. J. L. SHINE
Tim Haffigan	Mr. PERCIVAL STEVENS
Hodson	Mr. NIGEL PLAYFAIR
Keegan	Mr. GRANVILLE BARKER
Patsy Farrell	Mr. GRAHAM BROWNE
Father Dempsey	Mr. CHARLES DALY
Corney Doyle	Mr. F. CREMLIN
Barney Doran	Mr. WILFRED SHINE
Matthew Haffigan	Mr. A. E. GEORGE
Aunt Judy	Miss AGNES THOMAS
Nora	Miss ELLEN O'MALLEY

Act I.	Office of Broadbent & Doyle, Civil Engineers, Great George Street, Westminster.	
Act II.—Scene I.	Rosscullen Hill.	
Scene II.	The Round Tower.	
Act III.	The Grass Plot before Corney Doyle's House.	
Act IV.—Scene I.	The Parlour at Corney Doyle's.	
Scene II.	Rosscullen Hill.	

1904.

On November 15th, 17th, 18th, 22nd, 24th and
25th, at 2:30 p.m.

AGLAVAINE AND SELYSETTE

By Maeterlinck,
and translated by Alfred Sutro.

Aglavaine	...	...	...	... Miss EDYTH OLIVE
Selysette	...	...	...	.... Miss THYRZA NORMAN
Yssaline	...	...	...	... Miss MARION PLARR
Meligraine	...	...	...	... Miss FLORENCE FARR
Meleander	...	...	...	... Mr. WALTER HAMPDEN

The Incidental Music composed by Mr. DONALD TOVEY.

Orchestra under the direction of Mr. THEODORE STIER.

1904.

On November 29th, December 1st, 2nd, 6th,
8th, and 9th, at 3.

Extra Performances: Nov. 26th, at 3 and 8.30
Dec. 10th, at 3 and 8.30.

CANDIDA

By Bernard Shaw.

Candida	Miss KATE RORKE
Proserpine Garnett	Miss SYDNEY FAIR-BROTHER
The Rev. James Mavor Morell	Mr. C. V. FRANCE
Eugene Marchbanks	Mr. GRANVILLE BARKER
Mr. Burgess	Mr. EDWARD SASS
The Rev. Alexander Mill ...	Mr. ATHOL STEWART

The Action takes place at St. Dominic's Vicarage, Victoria
Park, E.

An October Day, 1894.

ACT I. Morning.   ACT II. Afternoon.   ACT III. Evening.

1904-5.

On December 23rd.

PRUNELLA
Or, Love in a Dutch Garden

A Play, in Three Acts, for Grown-up Children.
By Laurence Housman and Granville Barker.
The Music by Joseph Moorat.

Pierrot	Mr. GRANVILLE BARKER
Scaramel	Mr. HARRY DODD
Kennell	Mr. REGINALD RIVINGTON
Callow	Mr. JOHN W. DEVERELL
Mouth	Mr. ORLANDO BARNETT
Hawk	Mr. GEORGE TROLLOPE
Tawdry	Miss HELEN GRENVILLE
Doll	Miss MARGARET BUSSÉ
Romp	Miss FLORENCE REDFERN
Coquette	Miss HAZEL THOMPSON
Prim	Miss VIOLET VAUGHAN
Privacy	Miss NORA GREENLAW
Prude	Miss AGNES HILL
Queer	Miss EMILY GROVE
Quaint	Miss ALICE ARDEN
1st Gardener	Mr. TOM PAULTON
2nd Gardener	Mr. T. HESLEWOOD
3rd Gardener	Mr. F. CREMLIN
4th Gardener	Mr. F. GROVE
Boy	Mr. NORMAN PAGE
Statue of Love	Mr. LEWIS CASSON
Prunella	Miss THYRZA NORMAN

SCENE.—The Dutch Garden.
The Orchestra conducted by Mr. S. P. WADDINGTON.

1905.

On February 7th, 9th, 10th, 14th, 16th, 17th,
21st, 23rd, 24th, at 2.30 p.m.

[March 11, special evening performance for
H.M. the King.]

JOHN BULL'S OTHER ISLAND

By Bernard Shaw.

Broadbent	Mr. LOUIS CALVERT
Larry Doyle	Mr. C. M. HALLARD
Tim Haffigan	Mr. PERCIVAL STEVENS
Hodson	Mr. GEORGE TROLLOPE
Keegan	Mr. GRANVILLE BARKER
Patsy Farrell	Mr. NORMAN PAGE
Father Dempsey	Mr. J. D. BEVERIDGE
Corney Doyle	Mr. F. CREMLIN
Barney Doran	Mr. WILFRED SHINE
Matthew Haffigan	Mr. A. E. GEORGE
Aunt Judy	Miss AGNES THOMAS
Nora	Miss ELLEN O'MALLEY

ACT I.	Office of Broadbent & Doyle, Civil Engineers, Great George Street, Westminster.
ACT II.—Scene I.	Rosscullen Hill.
Scene II.	The Round Tower.
ACT III.	The Grass Plot before Corney Doyle's House.
ACT IV.—Scene I.	The Parlour at Corney Doyle's.
Scene II.	Rosscullen Hill.

1905.

On February 28th, March 2nd, 3rd, 7th, 9th,
10th, 14th, 16th, 17th, at 2.30 p.m.

THE POT OF BROTH

By W. B. Yeats.

John Coneely	Mr. GEORGE F. TULLY
Sibby Coneely	Miss AMY LAMBORN
A Tramp	Mr. ROBERT PATEMAN

IN THE HOSPITAL

By Arthur Schnitzler.

Translated by Christopher Horne.

Karl Rademacher	Mr. J. D. BEVERIDGE
Florian Schubart	Mr. GEORGE TROLLOPE
Alexander Weihgart	Mr. RUDGE HARDING
Dr. Lantner	Mr. HOWARD STURGE
Dr. Tann	Mr. EDMUND GWENN
Juliana Paschanda	Miss ISABEL GREY

SCENE.—An Extra Ward in the Vienna General Hospital.

HOW HE LIED TO HER HUSBAND

By Bernard Shaw.

Her Lover	Mr. GRANVILLE BARKER
Her Husband	Mr. A. G. POULTON
Herself	Miss GERTRUDE KINGSTON

SCENE.—Her Flat in Cromwell Road.

116 •

1905.

On March 21st, 23rd, 24th, 28th, 30th, 31st;

April 4th, 6th, 7th, at 2.30.

THE THIEVES' COMEDY

By Gerhart Hauptmann.

Translated by Christopher Horne.

Frau Wolff	Miss ROSINA FILIPPI
Frau Motes	Miss AGNES THOMAS
Adelheid	Miss SYDNEY FAIR-BROTHER
Leontine	Miss GRETA HAHN
Von Wehrhahn	Mr. W. LUGG
Kruger	Mr. WILLIAM FARREN, Junr.
Fleischer	Mr. HENRY VIBART
Motes	Mr. RUDGE HARDING
Julius Wolff	Mr. JAMES HEARN
Wulkoff	Mr. EDMUND GWENN
Glasenapp	Mr. NORMAN PAGE
Mitteldorf	Mr. HARRY DODD
Philip	Master TONGE

ACTS I. and III.   Frau Wolff's Cottage.

ACTS II. and IV.   The Magistrate's Office.

1905.

On April 11th, 13th, 14th, 18th, 20th, 25th,
27th, 28th, at 2.30.

THE TROJAN WOMEN OF EURIPIDES

Translated by Gilbert Murray.

The God Poseidon	Mr. CHARLES A. DORAN
The Goddess Pallas Athena	Miss ADA FERRAR
Hecuba	Miss MARIE BREMA
Cassandra	Miss EDYTH OLIVE
Andromache	Miss EDITH WYNNE-MATTHISON
Helen	Miss GERTRUDE KINGSTON
Talthybius	Mr. JAMES HEARN
Menelaus	Mr. DENNIS EADIE
Leader of the Chorus ...	Miss FLORENCE FARR

Chorus:

Mrs. BISHOP, Miss AMY LAMBORN,
Miss N. POWYS, Miss HAZEL THOMPSON,
Mrs. WHEELER, Miss MAUD YATES.

118 •

1905.

For Three Weeks Only.

Commencing on Monday, May 1st, 1905.

Every Evening at 8.15,

And Wednesday Matinée at 2.30.

JOHN BULL'S OTHER ISLAND

By Bernard Shaw.

Broadbent	Mr. LOUIS CALVERT
Larry Doyle	Mr. C. M. HALLARD
Tim Haffigan	Mr. A. G. POULTON
Hodson	Mr. NIGEL PLAYFAIR
Keegan	Mr. GRANVILLE BARKER
Patsy Farrell	Mr. NORMAN PAGE
Father Dempsey	Mr. J. D. BEVERIDGE
Corney Doyle	Mr. F. CREMLIN
Barney Doran	Mr. WILFRED SHINE
Matthew Haffigan	Mr. EDMUND GWENN
Aunt Judy	Miss AGNES THOMAS
Nora	Miss LILLAH McCARTHY

ACT I.	Office of Broadbent & Doyle, Civil Engineers, Great George Street, Westminster.
ACT II.—Scene I.	Rosscullen Hill.
Scene II.	The Round Tower.
ACT III.	The Grass Plot before Corney Doyle's House.
ACT IV.—Scene I.	The Parlour at Corney Doyle's.
Scene II.	Rosscullen Hill.

1905.

On May 2nd, 4th, 5th, 9th, 11th, 12th, 16th,
18th, 19th, at 2.30.

YOU NEVER CAN TELL

By Bernard Shaw.

Mrs. Clandon	...	... ...	Mrs. THEODORE WRIGHT
Gloria Clandon	...	... ...	Miss TITA BRAND
Dolly Clandon	...	... ...	Miss SYDNEY FAIRBROTHER
Philip Clandon	...	... ...	Mr. NORMAN PAGE
Fergus Crampton		... ...	Mr. J. D. BEVERIDGE
Finch McComas ...		... ...	Mr. J. H. BARNES
Valentine	...	... ...	Mr. GRANVILLE BARKER
Bohun ...	...	... ...	Mr. NIGEL PLAYFAIR
The Waiter ...	...	... ...	Mr. LOUIS CALVERT
A Parlour Maid	...	... ...	Miss HAZEL THOMPSON

ACT   I.   A Dentist's Operating Room—Morning.

ACT   II.   The Marine Hotel—Luncheon.

ACT III.   Sitting Room in the Hotel—Afternoon Tea.

ACT IV.   Sitting Room in the Hotel—After Dinner.

Scene.—At the Seaside.

Time.—The Present.

1905.

For Three Weeks Only.

Commencing on Monday, May 22nd, 1905.

Every Evening at 8.30,

And Wednesday Matinée at 3.

CANDIDA

By Bernard Shaw.

Candida	Miss KATE RORKE
Proserpine Garnett	Miss SYDNEY FAIR-BROTHER
The Rev. James Mavor Morell	Mr. C. V. FRANCE
Eugene Marchbanks	Mr. GRANVILLE BARKER
Mr. Burgess	Mr. A .G. POULTON
The Rev. Alexander Mill ...	Mr. HUBERT HARBEN

The Action takes place at St. Dominic's Vicarage, Victoria
Park, E.

An October Day, 1894.

Act I. Morning.   Act II. Afternoon.   Act III. Evening.

1905.

On May 23rd, 25th, 26th, 30th; June 1st, 2nd,
6th, 8th, 9th, 13th, 15th, 16th, at 2.30.

MAN AND SUPERMAN

By Bernard Shaw.

Roebuck Ramsden	... ...	Mr. CHARLES GOODHART
Octavius Robinson	... ...	Mr. LEWIS CASSON
John Tanner	... ...	Mr. GRANVILLE BARKER
Henry Straker	... ...	Mr. EDMUND GWENN
Hector Malone	... ...	Mr. HUBERT HARBEN
Mr. Malone ...	... ...	Mr. J. D. BEVERIDGE
Ann Whitefield	... ...	Miss LILLAH McCARTHY
Mrs. Whitefield	... ...	Miss FLORENCE HAYDON
Miss Ramsden	... ...	Miss AGNES THOMAS
Violet Robinson	... ...	Miss SARAH BROOKE
Parlour Maid	... ...	Miss HAZEL THOMPSON

ACT   I.   Portland Place. Roebuck Ramsden's Study.

ACT II.   Richmond. The Avenue to Mrs. Whitefield's House.

ACT III.   At Granada. The Villa Garden.

Period.—The Present Time.

122 •

1905.

For Three Weeks only.

Commencing on Monday, June 12th, 1905.

Every Evening at 8.15,

And Wednesday Matinée at 2.30.

YOU NEVER CAN TELL

By Bernard Shaw.

Mrs. Clandon	Mrs. THEODORE WRIGHT
Gloria Clandon	Miss TITA BRAND
Dolly Clandon	Miss S Y D N E Y F A I R-BROTHER
Philip Clandon	Mr. NORMAN PAGE
Fergus Crampton	Mr. J. D. BEVERIDGE
Finch McComas	Mr. J. H. BARNES
Valentine	Mr. GRANVILLE BARKER
Bohun	Mr. NIGEL PLAYFAIR
The Waiter	Mr. LOUIS CALVERT
A Parlour Maid	Miss HAZEL THOMPSON

ACT   I.   A Dentist's Operating Room—Morning.

ACT II.   The Marine Hotel—Luncheon.

ACT III.   Sitting Room in the Hotel—Afternoon Tea.

ACT IV.   Sitting Room in the Hotel—After Dinner.

Scene.—At the Seaside.

Time.—The Present.

1905.

Commencing on Monday, September 11th, 1905.

Every Evening at 8.15,

And Wednesday Matinée at 2.30.

JOHN BULL'S OTHER ISLAND

By Bernard Shaw.

Broadbent	Mr. LOUIS CALVERT
Larry Doyle	Mr. DANIEL McCARTHY
Tim Haffigan	Mr. EDMUND LEA
Hodson	Mr. EDMUND GWENN
Keegan	Mr. GRANVILLE BARKER
Patsy Farrell	Mr. NORMAN PAGE
Father Dempsey	Mr. J. H. BARNES
Corney Doyle	Mr. F. CREMLIN
Barney Doran	Mr. WILFRED SHINE
Matthew Haffigan	Mr. A. E. GEORGE
Aunt Judy	Miss AGNES THOMAS
Nora	Miss LILLAH McCARTHY

ACT I.	Office of Broadbent & Doyle, Civil Engineers, Great George Street, Westminster.
ACT II.—Scene I.	Rosscullen Hill.
Scene II.	The Round Tower.
ACT III.	The Grass Plot before Corney Doyle's House.
ACT IV.—Scene I.	The Parlour at Corney Doyle's.
Scene II.	Rosscullen Hill.

124 •

1905.

On September 26th, 29th; October 3rd, 6th,
10th, 13th, at 2.30.

THE RETURN OF THE PRODIGAL

A Comedy, in Four Acts, by St. John Hankin.

Samuel Jackson	Mr. J. H. BARNES
Mrs. Jackson	Miss FLORENCE HAYDON
Henry Jackson	Mr. DENNIS EADIE
Eustace Jackson	Mr. A. E. MATTHEWS
Violet Jackson	Miss AMY LAMBORN
Sir John Faringford, Bart. ...	Mr. ARTHUR APPLIN
Lady Faringford	Miss HILDA RIVERS
Stella Faringford	Miss HAZEL THOMPSON
Doctor Glaisher	Mr. F. W. PERMAIN
The Rev. Cyril Pratt	Mr. NORMAN PAGE
Mrs. Pratt	Miss AGNES THOMAS
Baines	Mr. EDMUND GWENN

The Action of the Play takes place at Chedleigh Court.

ACT   I.   The Drawing Room.

ACT II.   The Breakfast Room.

ACT III.   (Ten days have elapsed since Act II.) The Lawn.

ACT IV.   The Drawing Room.

1905.

On October 17th, 20th, 24th, 27th, 31st, and
November 3rd, at 2.30.

THE WILD DUCK

A Play, in Five Acts, by Henrik Ibsen.

Werle	Mr. OSCAR ADYE
Gregers Werle	Mr. SCOTT BUIST
Ekdal	Mr. A. E. GEORGE
Hialmar Ekdal	Mr. GRANVILLE BARKER*
Gina Ekdal	Miss AGNES THOMAS
Hedvig	Miss DOROTHY MINTO
Mrs. Sorby	Miss ADA FERRAR
Relling	Mr. MATHESON LANG
Molvik	Mr. NORMAN PAGE
Graberg	Mr. FREDERICK LLOYD
Pattersen	Mr. C. L. DELPH
Jensen	Mr. R. F. KNOX
Another Waiter	Mr. L. HAMER
Kasperen	Mr. EDMUND GWENN
Flor	Mr. KENELM F. FOSS
Balle	Mr. NORMAN PAGE
Another Gentleman	Mr. LEWIS CASSON

ACT I. Werle's Study.

ACTS II., III., IV., and V. Hialmar Ekdal's Studio.

---

*The part was played on Oct. 27th, 31st, and Nov. 3rd by Mr. Trevor
Lowe.

1905.

Commencing on Monday, October 23rd, 1905.

Every Evening at 8.15,

And Wednesday Matinée at 2.30.

MAN AND SUPERMAN

By Bernard Shaw.

Roebuck Ramsden ... ... Mr. J. H. BARNES
Octavius Robinson ... ... Mr. LEWIS CASSON
John Tanner ... ... Mr. GRANVILLE BARKER
Henry Straker ... . Mr. EDMUND GWENN
Hector Malone ... ... Mr. JAMES CAREW
Mr. Malone ... ... Mr. F. CREMLIN
Ann Whitefield ... ... Miss LILLAH McCARTHY
Mrs. Whitefield ... ... Miss FLORENCE HAYDON
Miss Ramsden ... ... Miss AGNES THOMAS
Violet Robinson ... ... Miss SARAH BROOKE
Parlour Maid ... ... Miss HAZEL THOMPSON

ACT I. Portland Place. Roebuck Ramsden's Study.

ACT II. Richmond. The Avenue to Mrs. Whitefield's House.

ACT III. At Granada. The Villa Garden.

Period.—The Present Time.

1905.

On November 7th, 10th, 14th, 17th, 21st, and
24th, at 2.30.

THE VOYSEY INHERITANCE

A Play, in Five Acts, by Granville Barker.

Mr. Voysey	Mr. A. E. GEORGE
Mrs. Voysey	Miss FLORENCE HAYDON
Trenchard Voysey, K.C. ...	Mr. EUGENE MAYEUR
Honor Voysey	Miss GERALDINE OLLIFFE
Major Booth Voysey ...	Mr. CHARLES FULTON
Mrs. Booth Voysey (Emily)	Miss GRACE EDWIN
Christopher	HARRY C. DUFF
Edward Voysey	Mr. THALBERG CORBETT
Hugh Voysey	Mr. DENNIS EADIE
Mrs. Hugh Voysey (Beatrice)	Miss HENRIETTA WATSON
Ethel Voysey	Miss ALEXANDRA CARLISLE
Denis Tregoning	Mr. FREDERICK LLOYD
Alice Maitland	Miss MABEL HACKNEY
Mr. Booth	Mr. O. B. CLARENCE
The Rev. Evan Colpus ...	Mr. EDMUND GWENN
Peacey	Mr. TREVOR LOWE
Phœbe	Miss GWYNNETH GALTON
Mary	Mrs. FORDYCE

ACTS I. and IV. At the Office of Voysey & Son, in
Lincoln's Inn.

ACTS II., III., and V. At Bramleyfield, Chislehurst.

128 •

1905.

On November 28th, December 1st, 5th, 8th,
12th, and 15th, at 2.30.

MAJOR BARBARA

A Discussion, in Three Acts, by Bernard Shaw.

Lady Britomart Undershaft	Miss ROSINA FILIPPI
Stephen Undershaft	Mr. HUBERT HARBEN
Morrison	Mr. C. L. DELPH
Barbara Undershaft	Miss ANNIE RUSSELL
Sarah Undershaft	Miss HAZEL THOMPSON
Charles Lomax	Mr. DAWSON MILWARD
Adolphus Cusins	Mr. GRANVILLE BARKER
Andrew Undershaft	Mr. LOUIS CALVERT
Rummy Mitchens	Miss CLARE GREET
Snobby Price	Mr. ARTHUR LACEBY
Jenny Hill	Miss DOROTHY MINTO
Peter Shirley	Mr. F. CREMLIN
Bill Walker	Mr. OSWALD YORKE
Mrs. Baines	Miss E. WYNNE-MATTHISON
Bilton	Mr. EDMUND GWENN

The characters are put in the order in which they
come on the stage.

Time.—Three successive days in **January, 1906.**
Place.—London.

Act I. ... ... The Library in Lady Britomart Undershaft's House in Wilton Crescent.

Act II. ... ... The West Ham Shelter of the Salvation
Army.

Act III. Scene I. The Library in Wilton Crescent.

Scene II. Among the high explosive Sheds at the
Arsenal of Messrs. Undershaft &
Lazarus, near the model town of
Perivale St. Andrews.

1906.
For Six Weeks Only.
Commencing on Monday, January 1st, 1906.
Every Evening at 8.15,
And Wednesday Matinée at 2.30.

MAJOR BARBARA

A Discussion, in Three Acts, by Bernard Shaw.

Lady Britomart Undershaft	Miss MADGE McINTOSH
Stephen Undershaft	Mr. HUBERT HARBEN
Morrison	Mr. C. L. DELPH
Sarah Undershaft	Miss HAZEL THOMPSON
Barbara Undershaft	Miss ANNIE RUSSELL
Charles Lomax	Mr. F. LUMSDEN HARE
Adolphus Cusins	Mr. LEWIS CASSON
Andrew Undershaft	Mr. LOUIS CALVERT
Rummy Mitchens	Miss CLARE GREET
Snobby Price	Mr. ARTHUR LACEBY
Jenny Hill	Miss DOROTHY MINTO
Peter Shirley	Mr. F. CREMLIN
Bill Walker	Mr. OSWALD YORKE
Mrs. Baines	Miss E. WYNNE-MATTHISON
Bilton	Mr. EDMUND GWENN

The characters are put in the order in which they
come on the stage.

Time.—Three successive days in January, 1906.
Place.—London.

ACT I. ... ... The Library in Lady Britomart Undershaft's House in Wilton Crescent.

ACT II. ... ... The West Ham Shelter of the Salvation
Army.

ACT III. Scene I. The Library in Wilton Crescent.
Scene II. Among the high explosive Sheds at the
Arsenal of Messrs. Undershaft &
Lazarus, near the model town of
Perivale St. Andrews.

NOTE.—Substituted with almost the same cast on February 13th, 16th,
20th, and 23rd, 1906, for *A Question of Age* and *The Convict on the
Hearth.*

130 •

1906.

On January 16th, 19th, 23rd, 26th, 30th,
and February 2nd, at 2.30.

THE ELECTRA OF EURIPIDES

Translated by Gilbert Murray.

The Scene is laid before a Peasant's Hut in the Mountains of
Argos. The Play was first acted in the year 413 B.C.

Electra (*Daughter of Agamemnon and Clytemnestra*)	Miss E. WYNNE-MATTHISON
Clytemnestra (*Queen of Argos, Widow of Agamemnon*)	Miss EDYTH OLIVE
Orestes (*Son of Agamemnon and Clytemnestra; now in banishment*) ...	Mr. E. HARCOURT WILLIAMS
A Peasant (*Husband of Electra*)	Mr. STRATTON RODNEY
An Old Man (*Formerly servant to Agamemnon*)	Mr. J. H. BARNES
A Messenger	Mr. HUBERT HARBEN
Pylades (*Son of Strophios, King of Phocis; friend to Orestes*)	Mr. FREDERICK LLOYD
Castor (*The demi-god, worshipped together with his twin brother Polydeuces*)	Mr. LEWIS CASSON
Leader of Chorus	Miss GERTRUDE SCOTT

Chorus:

Miss GWENDOLEN BISHOP, Miss AMY LAMBORN,
Miss VERA LONGDEN, Miss VIOLET MYERS,
Miss M. SAUMAREZ, Miss ELAINE SLEDDALL,
Miss HAZEL THOMPSON, Miss PENELOPE WHEELER.
Music by Theodore Stier.

NOTE.—Revived March 12th, 1906, for two weeks only, with the above
cast, except that Orestes was played by Mr. Henry Ainley.

1906.

On February 6th, 9th, [13th, 16th, 20th, and 23rd,]*
at 2.30.

A QUESTION OF AGE

A Comedy, in Three Acts, by Robert Vernon Harcourt.

Lt.-Col. Mark Langley, C.B.	Mr. FREDERICK KERR
Henry Bernard	Mr. C. M. HALLARD
Hon. Bertie Graham	Mr. KENNETH DOUGLAS
Baron von Berolstein ...	Mr. STRATTON RODNEY
Mr. Ferguson	Mr. FREDERIC TOPHAM
Johnson	Mr. C. L. DELPH
Footman	Mr. FREDERICK LLOYD
Mrs. Beddoes	Miss FANNY BROUGH
Olive Vane	Miss MABEL HACKNEY
Countess of Clare	Miss AGNES KNIGHTS
Lady Elsie Ireland	Miss IRENE FITZGERALD
Baroness von Berolstein ...	Miss DARRAGH
Shopwoman	Miss M. DANIELL
A Customer	Mrs. CHARLES MALTBY

ACT   I. Madame Lizette's Hat Shop, Dover Street.
ACT   II. The Hall at Lord Clare's, Steynham Court.
ACT III. Joint Rooms of Bernard & Graham, Park Place, St.
James.

To be followed by

THE CONVICT ON THE HEARTH
By Frederick Fenn.

George Midden	Mr. EDMUND GWENN
Thomas Midden	Mr. EDMUND GURNEY
Mrs. Midden	Miss MARY BROUGH
Jenny Midden	Miss EILY MALYON
Maud Midden	MERRIE OMAR
Percy Kitchener Midden ...	SIDNEY GRATA
Joseph Peterson	Mr. STRATTON RODNEY
Amy Watersmith	Miss CLARE GREET
Jim Watersmith	Mr. NORMAN PAGE
Miss Harcourt	Miss MADGE McINTOSH
Rev. Cartwright Dade ...	Mr. C. V. FRANCE

SCENE.—A Room in Corporation Buildings, Kennington Butts.

*Major Barbara was substituted for these four performances.

132 •

1906.

For Four Weeks only.

Commencing Monday, February 12th, 1906.

Every Evening at 8.15.

Wednesday Matinée at 2.30.

THE VOYSEY INHERITANCE

A Play, in Five Acts, by Granville Barker.

Mr. Voysey	Mr. FREDERICK KERR
Mrs. Voysey	Miss FLORENCE HAYDON
Trenchard Voysey, K.C. ...	Mr. EUGENE MAYEUR
Honor Voysey	Miss EDYTH OLIVE
Major Booth Voysey ...	Mr. CHARLES FULTON
Mrs. Booth Voysey (Emily)	Miss AMY LAMBORN
Christopher	CECIL DOYLE
Edward Voysey	Mr. GRANVILLE BARKER
Hugh Voysey	Mr. HUBERT HARBEN
Mrs. Hugh Voysey (Beatrice)	Miss MADGE McINTOSH
Ethel Voysey	Miss HAZEL THOMPSON
Denis Tregoning	Mr. FREDERICK LLOYD
Alice Maitland	Miss MABEL HACKNEY
Mr. Booth	Mr. NORMAN PAGE
The Rev. Evan Colpus ...	Mr. EDMUND GWENN
Peacey	Mr. TREVOR LOWE
Phœbe	Miss GWYNNETH GALTON
Mary	Mrs. CHARLES MALTBY

ACTS I. and IV. At the Office of Voysey & Son, in
Lincoln's Inn.

ACTS II., III., and V. At Bramleyfield, Chislehurst.

• 133

On Feb. 27th, Mar. 2nd, 6th, 9th, 13th, and 16th.

PAN AND THE YOUNG SHEPHERD

A Pastoral Play, in Two Acts, by Maurice Hewlett.
The Music by H. W. Hewlett.

Geron	Mr. EDMUND GURNEY
Neanias	Mr. HENRY AINLEY
Balkis	Miss RAY ROCKMAN
Teucer	Mr. NORMAN PAGE
Mopsus	Mr. EDMUND GWENN
Sphorx	Mr. STRATTON RODNEY
Merla	Miss SUZANNE SHELDON
Aglaë	Miss GRACE LANE
Erotion	Miss LILLAH McCARTHY
Sitys	Miss GWDENDOLEN BISHOP
Geërna	Miss HAZEL THOMPSON
Phoeno	Miss GWLADYS WYNNE
Dryas	Miss MABEL HACKNEY
Adora	Miss ALICE CRAWFORD
Pan	Mr. NORMAN McKINNEL

To be followed by

THE YOUNGEST OF THE ANGELS

By Maurice Hewlett.
Adapted by the Author from one of his Novels.

Dr. Dolfino Tron	Mr. J. H. BARNES
Mr. Francis Hastings ...	Mr. E. HARCOURT WILLIAMS
Donna Domenica	Miss LILLAH McCARTHY
Nonna	Miss AGNES THOMAS

1906.

On March 20th, 23rd, 27th, 30th; April 3rd
and 6th, at 2.30.

CAPTAIN BRASSBOUND'S CONVERSION

By Bernard Shaw.

Lady Cecily Waynflete	Miss ELLEN TERRY
Sir Howard Hallam	Mr. J. H. BARNES
Captain Brassbound	Mr. FREDERICK KERR
Rankin	Mr. F. CREMLIN
Drinkwater	Mr. EDMUND GWENN
Redbrook	Mr. C. L. DELPH
Johnson	Mr. EDMUND GURNEY
Marzo	Mr. MICHAEL SHER-BROOKE
Sidi el Assif	Mr. LEWIS CASSON
The Cadi	Mr. TREVOR LOWE
Osman	Mr. GORDON BAILEY
Hassan	Mr. JULES SHAW
Capt. Hamlin Kearney, U.S.N.	Mr. JAMES CAREW
American Bluejacket	Mr. FREDERICK LLOYD

ACT   I. Mogador. The Missionary's Garden.

ACT II. Moskala. In a Castle on the Hills.

ACT III. Mogador. In the Missionary's House.

NOTE.—Revived for twelve weeks on April 16th, 1906, with the above cast, and the additional character of *Muley*, played by Mr. Cecil Steel. The theatre was closed for one night, the day before Miss Ellen Terry's jubilee.

1906.

For Two Weeks only.

Commencing Monday, March 26th, 1906.

Every Evening at 8.30.
Wednesday Matinée at 2.30.

THE HIPPOLYTUS OF EURIPIDES

Translated by Gilbert Murray.

"The Play was first Acted when Epameinon was Archon, Olympiad 87, year 4 (429 B.C.). Euripides was first, Iophon second, Ion third."

The Goddess Aphrodite	Miss MADGE McINTOSH
The Goddess Artemis	Miss GWENDOLEN BISHOP
Theseus	Mr. WILLIAM HAVILAND
Hippolytus	Mr. HENRY AINLEY
Henchman	Mr. GRANVILLE BARKER
An Old Huntsman	Mr. STRATTON RODNEY
Phædra	Miss EDYTH OLIVE
The Nurse	Miss FLORENCE FARR
Leader of Chorus	Miss GERTRUDE SCOTT

Chorus of Trozenean Women.

Miss AMY LAMBORN, Miss VERA LONGDEN,
Miss VIOLET MYERS, Miss M. SAUMAREZ,
Miss ELAINE SLEDDALL, Miss HAZEL THOMPSON,
Miss PENELOPE WHEELER, Miss GWLADYS WYNNE.

SCENE.—Before Theseus' Castle in Trozen.
Music by FLORENCE FARR.

1906.

April 24th, 27th; May 1st, 4th, 8th, 11th,
15th, 18th, 22nd, 25th, 29th, and
June 1st, 1906, at 2.30.

PRUNELLA
Or, Love in a Dutch Garden

A Pierrot Play, in Three Acts,
By Laurence Housman and Granville Barker.

The Music by Joseph Moorat.

Pierrot	Mr. W. GRAHAM BROWNE
Scaramel	Mr. NIGEL PLAYFAIR
Kennel	Mr. TREVOR LOWE
Callow	Mr. GORDON BAILEY
Mouth	Mr. EDMUND GWENN
Hawk	Mr. C. H. CROKER-KING
Tawdry	Miss VALERIE SALBERG
Doll	Miss MARGARET BUSSÉ
Romp	Miss RUBY CRAWFORD
Coquette	Miss HAZEL THOMPSON
Tenor	Mr. W. H. PENDEREL PRICE
Prim	Mrs. CHARLES MALTBY
Privacy	Miss AMY LAMBORN
Prude	Miss AGNES HILL
Queer	Miss CLARE GREET
Quaint	Miss AGNES THOMAS
1st Gardener	Mr. C. L. DELPH
2nd Gardener	Mr. F. CREMLIN
3rd Gardener	Mr. EDMUND GURNEY
Boy	Mr. NORMAN PAGE
Statue of Love	Mr. LEWIS CASSON
Prunella	Miss DOROTHY MINTO

SCENE.—The Dutch Garden.
The Orchestra conducted by Mr. THEODORE STIER.

• 137

1906.

Commencing Monday, July 9th, 1906.
Every Evening at 8.15.
Wednesday Matinée at 2.30.
(For a Limited Number of Weeks.)

YOU NEVER CAN TELL

By Bernard Shaw.

Mrs. Clandon	...	... ...	Mrs. HENRIETTA WATSON
Gloria Clandon	...	... ...	Miss LILLAH McCARTHY
Dolly Clandon	...	... ...	Miss DOROTHY MINTO
Philip Clandon	...	... ...	Mr. NORMAN PAGE
Fergus Crampton		... ...	Mr. EDMUND GURNEY
Finch McComas	...	... ...	Mr. J. H. BARNES*
Valentine	... ...	... ...	Mr. HENRY AINLEY
Bohun ...	... ...	... ...	Mr. JAMES HEARN
The Waiter ...	...	... ...	Mr. LOUIS CALVERT
A Parlour Maid	...	... ...	Miss HAZEL THOMPSON

ACT   I.   A Dentist's Operating Room—Morning.
ACT II.   The Marine Hotel—Luncheon.
ACT III.   Sitting Room in the Hotel—Afternoon Tea.
ACT IV.   Sitting Room in the Hotel—After Dinner.

Scene.—At the Seaside.

Time.—The Present.

---

*When Mr. Barnes went out of the cast, the part was played by Mr. Athol Forde. In Mr. Calvert's absence the part of the Waiter was played by Mr. Edmund Gwenn; in Miss Minto's, the part of Dolly by Miss Margaret Bussé.

1906.

Monday, September 17th, for Six Weeks only.
Every Evening at 8.15.
Wednesday Matinée at 2.30.

JOHN BULL'S OTHER ISLAND

By Bernard Shaw.

Broadbent	Mr. LOUIS CALVERT
Larry Doyle	Mr. BEN WEBSTER
Tim Haffigan	Mr. HENRY AUSTIN
Hodson	Mr. EDMUND GWENN
Keegan	Mr. WILLIAM POEL
Patsy Farrell	Mr. NORMAN PAGE
Father Dempsey	Mr. EDMUND GURNEY
Corney Doyle	Mr. F. CREMLIN
Barney Doran	Mr. WILFRED SHINE
Matthew Haffigan	Mr. JAMES HEARN
Aunt Judy	Miss AGNES THOMAS
Nora	Miss ELLEN O'MALLEY

ACT   I.   ...   ...   Office of Broadbent & Doyle, Civil Engineers, Great George Street, Westminster.

ACT II.—Scene I.   Rosscullen Hill.

Scene II.   The Round Tower.

ACT III.   ...   ...   The Grass Plot before Corney Doyle's House.

ACT IV.—Scene I.   The Parlour at Corney Doyle's.

Scene II.   Rosscullen Hill.

1906.

On September 25th, 28th; October 2nd, 5th,
9th, 12th, 16th, 19th, at 2.30.

THE SILVER BOX

An Original Play, in Three Acts,

By John Galsworthy.

John Barthwick, M.P.	... Mr. JAMES HEARN
Jack Barthwick ...	... Mr. A. E. MATTHEWS
Mr. Roper	... Mr. A. GOODSALL
Marlow	... Mr. FREDERICK LLOYD
Jones	... Mr. NORMAN McKINNEL
Snow	... Mr. TREVOR LOWE
Julius Holden	... Mr. ATHOL FORDE
Livens	... Mr. EDMUND GURNEY
Magistrate's Clerk ...	... Mr. LEWIS CASSON
Relieving Officer ...	... Mr. EDMUND GWENN
Usher	... Mr. NORMAN PAGE
Mrs. Barthwick ...	... Miss FRANCES IVOR
Mrs. Jones	... Miss IRENE ROOKE
Mrs. Seddon	... Mrs. CHARLES MALTBY
Wheeler	... Miss GERTRUDE HENRIQUES
An Unknown Lady ...	... Miss SYDNEY FAIRBROTHER

ACT I. Easter Tuesday. The Dining Room at John Barthwick's, Rockingham Gate.

Scene I., 12.30 a.m. Scene II., 8.30 a.m. Scene III., 9 a.m.

ACT II. Scene I., The Jones' Lodgings, Merthyr Street. 2.30 p.m.

Scene II., The Dining Room. 8.30 p.m.

ACT III. A week later. A London Police Court. 1 p.m.

1906.

On October 23rd, 26th, 30th; November 2nd,
6th, 9th, 13th, 16th, at 2.30.

THE CHARITY THAT BEGAN AT HOME

A Comedy in Four Acts,

By St. John Hankin.

Lady Denison	Miss FLORENCE HAYDON
Margery	Miss MAY MARTYN
Mrs. Eversleigh	Miss MARGARET MURRAY
Mrs. Horrocks	Miss LIZZIE HENDERSON
Miss Triggs	Miss AGNES THOMAS
Anson	Miss GERTRUDE HEN-RIQUES
General Bonsor	Mr. DENNIS EADIE
Mr. Firket	Mr. EDMUND GWENN
Hugh Verreker	Mr. BEN WEBSTER
Basil Hylton	Mr. BERTE THOMAS
Soames	Mr. EUGENE MAYEUR
William	Mr. NORMAN PAGE

The action passes at Priors Ashton, Lady Denison's House in
the Country.

ACTS I., II., and III. The Drawing Room.
ACT IV. The Dining Room.

1906.

Monday, October 29th, 1906.
Every Evening at 8.15.
Wednesday Matinée at 2.30.

MAN AND SUPERMAN

By Bernard Shaw.

Roebuck Ramsden	Mr. JAMES HEARN
Octavius Robinson	Mr. LEWIS CASSON
John Tanner	Mr. GRANVILLE BARKER
Henry Straker	Mr. EDMUND GWENN
Hector Malone	Mr. HUBERT HARBEN
Mr. Malone	Mr. EDMUND GURNEY
Ann Whitefield	Miss LILLAH McCARTHY
Mrs. Whitefield	Miss FLORENCE HAYDON
Miss Ramsden	Miss AGNES THOMAS
Violet Robinson	Miss GRACE LANE
Parlour Maid	Miss MARY HAMILTON

ACT   I.   Portland Place. Roebuck Ramsden's Study.
ACT II.   Richmond. The Avenue to Mrs. Whitefield's House.
ACT III.   At Granada. The Villa Garden.

Period.—The Present Time.

1906.

On November 20th, 23rd, 27th, 30th;
December 4th, 7th, 11th, 14th, 1906,
at 2 o'clock.

THE DOCTOR'S DILEMMA *

A Tragedy, in Four Parts, and an Epilogue,

By Bernard Shaw.

Sir Patrick Cullen ... ... Mr. WILLIAM FARREN, Junr.
Sir Ralph Bloomfield
    Bonington ... ... Mr. ERIC LEWIS
Sir Colenso Ridgeon ... ... Mr. BEN WEBSTER
Cutler Walpole ... ... Mr. JAMES HEARN
Leo Schutzmacher ... ... Mr. MICHAEL SHERBROOKE
Dr. Blenkinsop ... ... Mr. EDMUND GURNEY
Louis Dubedat ... ... Mr. GRANVILLE BARKER
Redpenny ... ... Mr. NORMAN PAGE
The Newspaper Man ... ... Mr. TREVOR LOWE
Mr. Danby ... ... Mr. LEWIS CASSON
A Waiter ... ... Mr. PERCY MARMONT
Jennifer Dubedat ... ... Miss LILLAH McCARTHY
Emmy ... ... Miss CLARE GREET
Minnie Tinwell ... ... Miss MARY HAMILTON

ACT   I. Sir Colenso Ridgeon's Consulting Room, in Queen
        Anne Street, Portland Place, W.

ACT II. On the Terrace at "The Star and Garter," Richmond.

ACT III. Louis Dubedat's Studio.

ACT IV. The same.

Epilogue. A Bond Street Picture Gallery.

*The Doctor's Dilemma is the title of a story by Miss Hesba Stretton,
who has been kind enough to allow the Author to use it for his tragedy.

NOTE.—Revived on December 31st, 1906, for six weeks only, with the
above cast, except that The Newspaper Man was played by Mr. Jules
Shaw.

On January 8th, 11th, 15th, 18th, 22nd, 25th,
29th; February 1st, 1907, at 2.30.

THE REFORMER

A Very Light Comedy, in Three Acts,

by Cyril Harcourt.

Sir Rupert Yeld	Mr. ALLAN AYNESWORTH
The Earl of Crowborough	Mr. SYDNEY BROUGH
General Carew	Mr. O. B. CLARENCE
Captain Reginald Ross ...	Mr. JOHN L. MACKAY
Eric Lowndes	Mr. HUBERT HARBEN
Thomas	Mr. EDMUND GWENN
Ferrers	Mr. ALLAN WADE
Mrs. Rockingham	Miss EVA MOORE
Sybil Carew	Miss JUNE VAN BUSKIRK

ACTS I. and III. At General Carew's.
ACT II. Captain Ross's Chambers.

To be followed by

THE CAMPDEN WONDER

A Play, in Three Scenes, by John Masefield.

Mrs. Harrison	Miss DOLORES DRUMMOND
The Parson	Mr. EDMUND GURNEY
Mrs. Perry	Miss CARLOTTA ADDISON
John Perry	Mr. NORMAN McKINNEL
Richard Perry	Mr. H. R. HIGNETT
Tom Constable	Mr. NORMAN PAGE

Campden, Gloucestershire, 1660.

1907.

On February 5th, 8th, 12th, 15th, 19th, 22nd,
26th; March 1st, 1907, at 2.30.

THE PHILANDERER

A Topical Comedy, in Four Acts, of the early
Eighteen Nineties, by Bernard Shaw.

Leonard Charteris	Mr. BEN WEBSTER
Mrs. Grace Tranfield	Miss WYNNE-MATTHISON
Julia Craven	Miss MARY BARTON
Colonel Daniel Craven, V.C.	Mr. ERIC LEWIS
Mr. Joseph Cuthbertson ...	Mr. LUIGI LABLACHE
Sylvia Craven	Miss DOROTHY MINTO
Dr. Paramore	Mr. HUBERT HARBEN
The Club Page	Mr. CYRIL BRUCE

Period.—During the first vogue of Ibsen in London after 1889.

ACT I. Mr. Joseph Cuthbertson's Flat in Ashley Gardens.

ACTS II. and III. The Library of the Ibsen Club in Cork Street.

ACT IV. Dr. Paramore's Rooms in Savile Row.

1907.

Commencing Monday, February 11th, 1907,
For Six Weeks only.
Every Evening at 8.15,
Wednesday Matinée at 2.30.

YOU NEVER CAN TELL

By Bernard Shaw.

Mrs. Clandon ...	... ...	Miss HENRIETTA WATSON
Gloria Clandon ...	... ...	Miss GRACE LANE
Dolly Clandon ...	... ...	Miss DOROTHY MINTO
Philip Clandon ...	... ...	Mr. NORMAN PAGE
Fergus Crampton	... ...	Mr. EDMUND GURNEY
Finch McComas	... ...	Mr. ATHOL FORDE
Valentine	... ...	Mr. GRANVILLE BARKER
Bohun	... ...	Mr. JAMES HEARN
The Waiter ...	... ...	Mr. LOUIS CALVERT
A Parlour Maid	... ...	Miss PENELOPE WHEELER

ACT   I.   A Dentist's Operating Room—Morning.
ACT   II.   The Marine Hotel—Luncheon.
ACT III.   Sitting Room in the Hotel—Afternoon Tea.
ACT IV.   Sitting Room in the Hotel—After Dinner.

Scene.—At the Seaside.

Time.—The Present.

NOTE.—Continued on April 1st, 1907, for seven extra performances.

146 •

1907.

On March 5th, 8th, 12th, 15th, 19th, 22nd, 26th,
1907, at 2.30.

HEDDA GABLER

A Play, in Four Acts,

By Henrik Ibsen.

Hedda Tesman	Mrs. PATRICK CAMPBELL
Mrs. Elvsted	Miss EVELYN WEEDEN
Miss Juliana Tesman	Miss ADELA MEASOR
Berta	Miss MARY RABY
George Tesman	Mr. TREVOR LOWE
Judge Brack	Mr. JAMES HEARN
Eilert Lövborg	Mr. LAURENCE IRVING

The Scene of the Action is Tesman's Villa in the
West End of Christiania.

1907.

Monday, April 8th, for Three Weeks only.

Every Evening at 8.30,
Wednesday Matinée at 2.30.

THE SILVER BOX

An Original Play, in Three Acts,

By John Galsworthy.

John Barthwick, M.P. ...	Mr. JAMES HEARN
Jack Barthwick	Mr. A. E. MATTHEWS
Mr. Roper	Mr. CECIL ROSE
Marlow	Mr. DENNIS EADIE
Jones	Mr. NORMAN McKINNEL
Snow	Mr. TREVOR LOWE
The Magistrate	Mr. ATHOL FORDE
The Magistrate's Clerk ...	Mr. LEWIS CASSON
Livens	Mr. EDMUND GURNEY
Relieving Officer	Mr. EDMUND GWENN
Usher	Mr. NORMAN PAGE
Mrs. Barthwick	Miss FRANCES IVOR
Mrs. Jones	Miss NORA GREENLAW
Mrs. Seddon	Mrs. CHARLES MALTBY
Wheeler	Miss AMY LAMBORN
An Unknown Lady	Miss MARY HAMILTON

ACT I. Easter Tuesday. The Dining Room at John Barthwick's, Rockingham Gate.

Scene I., 12.30 a.m. Scene II., 8.30 a.m. Scene III., 9 a.m.

ACT II. Scene I., The Jones' Lodgings, Merthyr Street, 2.30 p.m.

Scene II., The Dining Room. 8.30 p.m.

ACT III. A week later. A London Police Court. 12.15 p.m.

148 •

1907.

On April 9th, 12th, 16th, 19th, 23rd, 26th, 30th,
and May 3rd, 1907, at 2.30.

VOTES FOR WOMEN!

A Dramatic Tract in Three Acts,

By Elizabeth Robins.

Lord John Wynnstay ...	Mr. ATHOL FORDE
The Hon. Geoffrey Stonor	Mr. AUBREY SMITH
Mr. St. John Greatorex ...	Mr. E. HOLMAN CLARK
Mr. Richard Farnborough ...	Mr. P. CLAYTON GREENE
Mr. Freddy Tunbridge ...	Mr. PERCY MARMONT
Mr. Allen Trent	Mr. LEWIS CASSON
Mr. Walker	Mr. EDMUND GWENN
Lady John Wynnstay ...	Miss MAUD MILTON
Mrs. Heriot	Miss FRANCES IVOR
Miss Vida Levering	Miss WYNNE-MATTHISON
Miss Beatrice Dunbarton ...	Miss JEAN MacKINLAY
Mrs. Freddy Tunbridge ...	Miss GERTRUDE BURNETT
Miss Ernestine Blunt ...	Miss DOROTHY MINTO
A Working Woman	Miss AGNES THOMAS

ACT I. Wynnstay House in Hertfordshire.

ACT II. Trafalgar Square, London.

ACT III. Eaton Square, London.

The Entire Action of the Play takes place between Sunday
noon and six o'clock in the evening of the same day.

NOTE.—Substituted for two weeks only, beginning May 11th, 1907, in
place of *The Return of the Prodigal*, with the same cast as above.

1907.

April 29th, 1907 (for Four Weeks only).
Every Evening at 8.30.
Wednesday Matinée at 2.30.

THE RETURN OF THE PRODIGAL

A Comedy, in Four Acts, by St. John Hankin.

Samuel Jackson	Mr. ERIC LEWIS
Mrs. Jackson	Miss FLORENCE HAYDON
Henry Jackson	Mr. DENNIS EADIE
Eustace Jackson	Mr. A. E. MATTHEWS
Violet Jackson	Miss AMY LAMBORN
Sir John Faringford, Bart. ...	Mr. CECIL ROSE
Lady Faringford	Miss FORTESCUE
Stella Faringford	Miss DOROTHY MINTO
Doctor Glaisher	Mr. JAMES HEARN
The Rev. Cyril Pratt	Mr. NORMAN PAGE
Mrs. Pratt	Miss MARY BARTON
Baines	Mr. EDMUND GWENN

The Action of the Play takes place at Chedleigh Court.

Act   I.   The Drawing Room.
Act   II.   The Breakfast Room.
Act   III.   The Lawn. Ten days have elapsed since Act II.
Act   IV.   The Drawing Room.

NOTE.—On May 10th, *Votes for Women!* was substituted for this play.

150 •

1907.

On May 7th, 10th, 14th, 17th, 21st, 24th,
28th, 31st, 1907, at 2.30.

PRUNELLA
Or, Love in a Dutch Garden

A Pierrot Play, in Three Acts,
By Laurence Housman and Granville Barker.
Music by Joseph Moorat.

Pierrot	Mr. W. GRAHAM BROWNE
Scaramel	Mr. JAMES HEARN
Kennel	Mr. TREVOR LOWE
Callow	Mr. ALLAN WADE
Mouth	Mr. EDMUND GWENN
Hawk	Mr. KENELM FOSS
Tawdry	Miss DOROTHY MARSDEN
Doll	Miss MARGARET BUSSÉ
Romp	Miss MARY HAMILTON
Coquette	Miss HAZEL THOMPSON
A Light Baritone	Mr. JULIEN HENRY
Prim	Mrs. CHARLES MALTBY
Privacy	Miss AMY LAMBORN
Prude	Miss AGNES HILL
Queer	Miss CLARE GREET
Quaint	Miss AGNES THOMAS
First Gardener	Mr. JULES SHAW
Second Gardener	Mr. F. CREMLIN
Third Gardener	Mr. EDMUND GURNEY
Boy	Mr. NORMAN PAGE
Statue of Love	Mr. LEWIS CASSON
Prunella	Miss DOROTHY MINTO

SCENE.—The Dutch Garden.

The Orchestra conducted by Mr. THEODORE STIER.

1907.

Monday, May 27th, for Five Weeks only.
Every Evening at 8.30,
Wednesday Matinée at 2.30.

MAN AND SUPERMAN

By Bernard Shaw.

Roebuck Ramsden	... ...	Mr. JAMES HEARN
Octavius Robinson	... ...	Mr. LEWIS CASSON
John Tanner	... ...	Mr. ROBERT LORAINE
Henry Straker	... ...	Mr. EDMUND GWENN
Hector Malone	... ...	Mr. DENNIS EADIE
Mr. Malone ...	... ...	Mr. EDMUND GURNEY
Ann Whitefield	... ...	Miss LILLAH McCARTHY
Mrs. Whitefield	... ...	Miss FLORENCE HAYDON
Miss Ramsden	... ...	Miss AGNES THOMAS
Violet Robinson	... ...	Miss SARAH BROOKE
Parlour Maid	... ...	Miss MARY HAMILTON

Act   I.   Portland Place. Roebuck Ramsden's Study.
Act II.   Richmond. The Avenue to Mrs. Whitefield's House.
Act III.   At Granada. The Villa Garden.

Period.—The Present Time.

1907.

On June 4th, 7th, 11th, 14th, 18th, 21st, 25th, 28th, 1907, at 2.30.

DON JUAN IN HELL

A Dream, from Man and Superman,

By Bernard Shaw.

Don Juan ... ... Mr. ROBERT LORAINE
Dona Ana de Ulloa ... ... Miss LILLAH McCARTHY
The Statue ... ... Mr. MICHAEL SHERBROOKE
The Devil ... ... Mr. NORMAN McKINNEL

SCENE.—Beyond Space.　　　PERIOD.—Beyond Time.
The Costumes designed by Mr. Charles Ricketts.

To be followed by

THE MAN OF DESTINY

A Trifle by Bernard Shaw.

General Bonaparte ... ... Mr. DION BOUCICAULT
Giuseppe (the Innkeeper) Mr. HERMAN DE LANGE
A Lieutenant ... ... Mr. TREVOR LOWE
The Strange Lady ... ... Miss IRENE VANBRUGH

PERIOD.—May 12th, 1796.

SCENE.—Interior of a Farmhouse at Tavazzano in North
Italy, on the road from Lodi to Milan.

TIME.—7.30 in the Evening.

• 153

APPENDIX II

The Complimentary Dinner to
Mr. J. E. Vedrenne and Mr. H. Granville **Barker:**
A transcript of the proceedings

Before their partnership ended, Vedrenne and Barker moved from the Court to the Savoy Theatre in The Strand to produce an historic season of Shakespeare under Barker's direction. Just prior to this, at the close of the final Court season, a group of actors, authors, and devotees of the theatre organized a testimonial dinner to honor Barker and Vedrenne, the committee consisting of William Archer, James Barrie, Sir Hugh and Lady Bell, John Galsworthy, J. T. Grein, Robert Harcourt, G. C. Ashton-Jonson, W. Lee Mathews, Gilbert Murray, John Pollock, Charles Ricketts, Robert Ross, Mr. and Mrs. G. Bernard Shaw, J. A. Spender, Alfred Sutro, W. Hector Thomson, H. Beerbohm Tree, and Frederick Whelen. For Shaw's benefit there was a vegetarian menu in addition to the regular menu, including Omlette Chatelaine, Tomato Forestiere, Macaroni au Gratin, *and* Pommes Maria. *Invitations were accepted by more than three hundred men and women, and the dinner was held at the Criterion Restaurant on July 7, 1907. The toasts began with the traditional one to King Edward VII. Subsequent proceedings were recorded in the now-rare "Souvenir" book* of the occasion, and provide a footnote as well as a conclusion to the history of the Vedrenne-Barker seasons at the Court.*

The Chairman, Lord Lytton, in proposing the "Health of the Guests of the Evening," said:—

Ladies and Gentlemen,—I now ask you to pledge the health of our two guests, the heroes of the evening, Mr. Vedrenne and Mr. Barker. I ought, perhaps, to explain that this dinner is the outcome of a spontaneous desire on the part of many of those who have found real pleasure and entertainment in the performances at the Court Theatre during the last three years, to express to Mr. Vedrenne and Mr. Barker their gratitude and appreciation in some public manner. We are here tonight to tell these two gentlemen of our admiration for their perform-

---

*Reprinted here from *The Shaw Review*, May 1959, pp. 17-34, which utilized the copy in the collection of LaFayette Butler. The speech by G.B.S. was reprinted separately in *Platform and Pulpit*, ed. Dan H. Laurence (New York, 1961), pp. 36-41.

ances at the Court Theatre, and of the high hopes with which we look forward to their future efforts at the Savoy.

You, ladies and gentlemen have probably, all of you, very lively recollections of many a delightful afternoon and evening spent at the Court Theatre—occasions of real intellectual pleasure, which is an experience not too frequent nowadays— and you therefore know, far better than I can express, how great is the debt of gratitude which every lover of the drama owes to our two guests. They have rescued English drama from the chains of a stupid convention by which it has long been bound. They have never tried to run their plays to death, and have resisted the temptation of making as much as possible out of a popular play. Mr. Bernard Shaw will, I hope, forgive me if I remind him that his plays were sometimes in great danger of becoming popular, but he was saved by Messrs. Vedrenne and Barker, because as soon as one of his plays began to be thoroughly appreciated it was promptly removed from the stage. These two gentlemen have ignored the supposed taste of the public, and set up for themselves a different standard of merit. They have chosen plays which in their own opinion possessed some real intellectual interest or artistic merit, and they have got them acted in a truly admirable man- ner. In short, they have done what every genuine artist always does: they have pursued their art for its own sake, and not for the sake of what it may bring them. And what has been the result? They have achieved a remarkable and richly-de- served success. Like Solomon, they elected wisdom rather than riches, excellence rather than popularity; and, like him, they have found that all other things have been added unto them.

When I say that they have achieved success, I don't merely mean that they have had full houses and favourable notices in the press—though no actor-manager could be indifferent to such things—these they have had, no doubt, but if our two guests are the genuine artists which I believe them to be, there are other features of their three years' experiment at the Court Theatre which must give them greater pleasure. They have proved that apart from what I may call the stars of their profession this country is capable of producing at the present day both dramatic writing and acting of the very highest order. They have shown that Mr. Shaw's plays are no less brilliant on the stage than they are to read, and that the Greek tragedies of Euripides, when translated by the master hand and the poetic genius of Mr. Gilbert Murray, can delight an English audience. In addition to these two authors who have been the chief contributors, there have been many others of great interest, such, for instance, as Mr. Galsworthy's *Silver Box* and Mr. Barker's own *Voysey Inheritance*. Speaking of my own experience, I can say that I have often felt extremely reluctant to leave London lest I should miss something really good at the Court Theatre. Perhaps you, too, ladies and gentlemen, have felt the same thing, and, if so, then, we may say fairly that Mr. Vedrenne and Mr. Barker have taken away that reproach which one so often hears that to see really good acting it is necessary to cross the channel. They have given us something as good as can be found in any other country, something of which, as Englishmen, we can be justly proud.

In saying this, I don't wish to suggest that the authors and actors of the Court Theatre have a monopoly of dramatic talent and that no good acting is to be found elsewhere. But all other theatres have this common defect, that their plays are intended to run. The expense and trouble which is involved in their productions necessitate their being produced for a great many nights in succession. This system not only prevents a great many plays from being acted at all—plays which may have great intellectual interest but which could not have a long life, but it also tends to destroy the artistic effect of the plays which are acted. It was its departure from this tradition which differentiated the Court Theatre from all other theatres and which gave to it its special interest. We are met here tonight to honour Mr. Vedrenne and Mr. Barker, not merely because they have given us good plays and good acting, but because they have tried successfully a new system of management and introduced a new element into the English drama.

Ladies and gentlemen, we are a very conservative people in this country. Perhaps you may doubt the truth of this, and I admit that there are elements in the composition of the present

House of Commons which seem to suggest a different conclusion. But the fact is that the House of Commons itself is an intensely conservative body. It has in a marked degree that intense belief in its own excellence which is the hallmark of conservatism. It matters not how it is composed nor what may be the character of the speeches delivered in it. Under varying conditions it still remains a conservative body. And, as with the House of Commons, so it is with the English people. We are slow to take up a new cause until we are sure that it is a winning one; we prefer practice and experience to theories, however plausible, and we are intensely reluctant to imitate the example of other countries. This may be seen, not only in our institutions and our habits, but also in our theatrical system. The long-run system may be bad in theory, the arguments against it may be overwhelming, the experience of other countries may point to an alternative, but it is necessary, before any change can be effected, for some individual to make an experiment and prove its success. Messrs. Vedrenne and Barker have supplied such an experiment as was wanted, and have proved, I think, the direction in which reform is needed. It is true that the Court Theatre was not a true repertory theatre, but it was a step in that direction, and it was successful just in proportion as it departed from the long-run system and approached the repertory system. The actors themselves seemed to have realised the change, for one of the most remarkable features of the performances at the Court was the uniformly excellent quality of the acting. In every case the performers seem to have shown their highest qualities. I cannot believe that it will be long before the next step is taken and we meet together again to congratulate our two guests of tonight on the completion of their experiment in the establishment of a real National Repertory Theatre.

Ladies and gentlemen, I have only one word to say in conclusion as to the future, for in drinking the health of our two guests we are drinking to their future success. There seem to me to be only two dangers ahead. One of them is a danger which concerns them, and against which they alone can guard. The other concerns us, and it is for us to prevent it. First, then, I fear lest Mr. Vedrenne and Mr. Barker should become too popular, and as a result of their popularity they should seek to please too many people. The man who tries to please everybody will end by despising himself and pleasing no one. The business of an artist is to please himself, and any one who comes within measurable distance of doing that will, if he is a true artist, succeed in pleasing the whole world. If our two guests will but follow the lines which they have already laid down and keep strictly to their own ideals, I have no fears for their future success.

The second danger is that we may be slow to learn the lessons which the Vedrenne-Barker management has been trying to teach us, and that in our reluctance to make use of their experience, another nation, less conservative than ourselves, more watchful for any exhibition of talent, and more ready to reward it, may slip in and do what we have not done. In short, I fear lest America may rob us of Mr. Barker. If we do not provide him soon with a repertory theatre in England he will be summoned to manage one in the United States. Such a calamity we must prevent if we can, for to allow Mr. Barker's talents to be bought by another country would be a severe blow to the English drama and an abiding disgrace to this country.

Mr. J. E. Vedrenne in replying, said:—

I want to thank you, to thank you all for the honour that you are doing my partner and myself this evening. I also thank our chairman and the ladies and gentlemen of the committee who have so very kindly organised this gathering. It is an evening that Barker and I will never forget, and we are proud to think that you thought us worthy of this special recognition. I want to take this occasion to thank publicly all those who have helped us to build whatever reputation we may have obtained; first, the authors who have given us the plays, and the actors and actresses who have so loyally worked with us.

Then the staff, especially those humbler members whom the public never see. I also want to specially thank our brother managers for their valuable help in lending us artists for our special matinees, and last but not least the press, for the large amount of attention which was devoted to our work; but above all we want to thank you all for your support in the past and trust that we shall please you again in the future.

Mr. H. Granville Barker in replying, said:—

Lord Lytton, ladies and gentlemen.—It is very good of you to have asked us to dinner. Vedrenne and I have never, so to speak, been asked out to dinner before. I feel though, not so much as if I was at dinner, as at a meeting of shareholders, for I think your kindness shows that I may term you at least moral shareholders in our enterprise. And it is my duty, not so much to thank you again, as to report to you on the work we have done and tried to do. As far as the artistic part of it goes, we must never forget that we are standing on the shoulders of other men. Our work is but a continuation of that begun by Mr. Grein and the Independent Theatre, and carried on by Mr. Archer and the New Century Theatre, and by that body to which I am always inclined to refer as my father and mother called the Stage Society. Don't let us forget, either, though on a side issue, the contributions that Mr. William Poel and the Elizabethan Stage Society have made to the modern history of the English Theatre. But what I think may ultimately be found to have been significant in our enterprise is the method on which we have produced our plays. I feel very strongly, as I think everyone must, the necessity for a change in the English theatrical system. To my mind no drama and no school of acting can long survive the strangling effects of that boa-constrictor, the long run. What is needed, of course, is a repertory theatre, but the difficulty of establishing one in London would be very great, greater than Lord Lytton thinks. As a good Socialist I am glad to be able to sum up the chief of those difficulties in the one word rent. The theatre manager cannot stand up against the ground landlord. Therefore, and as a Londoner, I sincerely regret it, I think we must look for the first repertory theatre of the new order in Manchester or Birmingham, or some such centre where either the price of land is not so enormous or where the municipality or some public body will have public spirit enough to nullify this diffi-

culty. At the Court we have by no means started a repertory
theatre or anything like it, but we have introduced a system
which may prove the artistic necessity of such institution. We
have opposed to the long run system the short run system. It
has many disadvantages, perhaps, but it keeps the plays fresh,
and from a business point of view it is perfectly justifiable, as
you will see when I report to you the total number of performances of some of our plays. *You Never Can Tell* attained
to 149, *John Bull's Other Island* to 121, *Man and Superman*
to 176. Well, though these records might be just as good and
far more satisfactory in a repertory theatre, I think we may
claim that the plays are more alive now both from a business
and an artistic point of view, than they would have been had
they simply been run callously to the fullest limit of their
popularity. It is surely almost unnecessary for us to insist on
the debt which we owe both to authors and to actors. First
among the authors comes, of course, Bernard Shaw, who I may
say has been more than an author to us, he has been an inspiration. I might call him the goose that has laid the golden eggs,
if I could not find another more suitable metaphor by thinking
of him as our Ugly Duckling. By a curious fate I was, long
before the days of the Court Theatre, connected in one way or
another with almost every play of his, and it will always be
a pride to me to remember that even then I was able to discern
beneath the down the Swan of Adelphi Terrace. There follows
a long list of those to whom we owe much thanks. *Euripides*, in
the person of Gilbert Murray, by whose plays I have been
taught so much, St. John Hankin, John Galsworthy, John
Masefield, Laurence Housman, Maurice Hewlett, Frederick
Fenn, Robert Harcourt, Cyril Harcourt—I have even now not
named them all; and as to the actors, if I once began about
them, I should find it difficult to stop. If they will allow me one
remark, I would rather think of them as a company than as
individuals, brilliant individually as they may be, for I feel
very strongly that it is the playing together of a good company which makes good performances. Even here in Mr. Tree's
presence, and all the more perhaps, in his presence, I cannot
resist throwing a stone at the actor manager. I say all the
more in his presence, because it must not be thought, as it is

thought by many detractors, that the actor manager is an egotistical person who stands in the center of the stage to let his company revolve round him. More often he is so occupied in getting the best work out of other actors, and with the many troubles of a production, that he is unable to get the best work out of himself. I do not believe that it is possible for a man to play his best and produce his best at the same time. The actor manager is the victim of what is, to my mind, a vicious system. The wind was sown long ago when productions were not perhaps the complicated things they now are, and in our times the whirlwind is being reaped. Perhaps I shall be accused of being the thing I decry, but it will have been noticed by those who are very familiar with the Court Theatre that I act almost exclusively in Bernard Shaw's plays, and Bernard Shaw produces his plays himself. Moreover, if they had ever heard Mr. Shaw giving me before the assembled company his opinion of my performances, they would recognise that no egotism would long survive it. I am happy to think that the play and the company as a whole have almost always been the attraction at the Court Theatre. I remember that during one of the revivals of *Man and Superman*, in which I was playing John Tanner, (I have by the way, been able to enjoy that play for the first time lately in watching Mr. Robert Loraine in that part)—well, I caught influenza and was out of the bill for a night or two. A gentleman descending the pit stairs observed a notice to this effect pinned above the pay box. He asked what it meant, and it was carefully explained that Mr. Barker was not playing that evening. "Who is Barker?" he asked. The money-taker did not commit himself to a biography, but repeated that Mr. Barker would not play John Tanner. "But I suppose somebody will play it," said the gentleman. "Yes," said the money-taker, "it will be played." "Then," said the gentleman, "take my half-crown, young man, and don't make such a fuss." Now, I think that is a proper spirit in which to go to the theatre. It is the spirit, I think, in which most of our audiences came to the Court, and in that spirit I hope they will come to the Savoy. We seem to have a fair amount of work to do there—a new play by Galsworthy, another by Housman and Moorat—one of my own, in which Vedrenne expresses a touching belief (I may remark that he has not yet read it), another translation from *Euripides*, a new play by Mr. Shaw, and lastly, we mean to attempt to the best of our ability a production of Ibsen's *Peer Gynt*.

Mr. Beerbohm Tree in proposing the toast, "The Authors of the Court Theatre," said.—

There are two sides to most questions. There is a certain appropriateness, as there is a certain inappropriateness, in the selection of myself to propose this toast. There are many present who are more intimately acquainted than I with the work of the Court Theatre authors—there are many who would express themselves in terms of more eloquent eulogy than is given to me. But in one sense there is none better fitted to propose this toast, for I rank myself second to none in sympathy with the work done by our guests, and in admiration of the admirable record, to do honour to which this distinguished assembly is gathered tonight.

Ladies and gentlemen, there is one great advantage to be derived from a careful perusal of the newspapers, for the contradiction of their inaccuracies always supplies a useful jumping-board for a speech. I will begin with a contradiction. I read in an important daily paper that I was to propose the toast of the author of the Court Theatre. Well, ladies and gentlemen, this is not strictly accurate, for although Mr. Bernard Shaw is a host in himself, "there are others," as Mr. Archer once observed in a moment of literary aberration. It is the toast of "The Authors of the Court" that it is my privilege to propose, for the happy realisation of high endeavour which we are celebrating tonight is, of course, in a large measure, due to the band of writers who have gathered together in that little temple of art called the Court Theatre. But it is appropriate that that remarkable man—I was almost saying that remarkable institution—known as Bernard Shaw, should be the spokesman of this distinguished band, for to him more than any other belongs the literary godfathership of the Court Theatre. It is only right that he, the head and front of its offending, should be given an opportunity of explaining himself, if he can. To be understood is to be found out. Of course, it is always difficult for a community of Englishmen to understand an Irishman. It is this lack of alertness in the Saxon race which explains its difficulty in governing the Irish people. Of course, some there are who cannot take Mr. Shaw seriously because he is humorous; there are other who cannot see his humour because he is serious. This mental agility, which is a characteristically Irish possession, is often disconcerting to us heavy-minded Saxons. The most searching criticism of our times on Ireland and on Irish national character is contained in a play written by Bernard Shaw, called *John Bull's Other Island*. Here it seems to me, he showed that impartiality of the literary artist, that serenity of outlook, which towers him above the minor thinkers of our age. Before I leave this subject—and it is difficult to escape Bernard Shaw —it has been the vain endeavour of my life to do so—so all-pervading is he, that he cannot even escape from himself. But before leaving him to himself I should like to take this opportunity of correcting another misstatement in the press, with which his name is connected. I read yesterday that three great men had foregathered at luncheon—they were Mark Twain, Bernard Shaw, and Beerbohm Tree. It was said that the conversation was most brilliant. Ladies and gentlemen, I believe the conversation was most brilliant, although I was not there. As some of my brilliant flourishes of silence may be recorded in the newspapers, I think it only right to give credit where credit is due. I believe the distinction belonged to my brother, Max Beerbohm. Now, he is not a brilliant conversationalist, but I have never known so witty a listener, and it was probably in this capacity that he commended himself to the hospitality of Bernard Shaw and Mark Twain. In passing, I may pay a little tribute to my relative, for if one cannot praise oneself it is always pleasant to the egotist to speak of his family. My little story shows how early in life the literary faculty asserts itself. I remember Max showed this faculty in an extraordinary degree on the occasion of his tenth birthday, when I had occasion to admonish him for too liberally drinking his own health in champagne cup. Even in his then deplorable condition the budding literary artist proclaimed himself. "Max," I said, in my most portentous manner, "it is bad to be tipsy at ten." He retorted upon me with that customary literary *riposte*, with that grace of style which has made English famous among the languages. Here are his memorable words: "How can one be tipsy when we are conscious they are not?" Oh, how I envy this literary gift—the power to select words that will make a sentence vibrate through the ages!

But I must return to my *leit-motif*—my song of praise of the authors of the Court Theatre. That institution in its three years of existence has had many authors, and several of them, I am glad to see, are here this evening. In glancing round the room my eye falls on Mr. Gilbert Murray, who has the proud distinction of being the first author whose work was produced under the management whom we are met here to honour this evening. I refer to Mr. Murray's translation of *The Hippolytus of Euripides*. It may be objected that the play was by Euripides, and not by Gilbert Murray. I admit that the objection has the element of truth in it, but all who know the fineness of the work done by Mr. Murray in his translations will ungrudgingly pardon me in my reference to him. In glancing through the list of plays I notice that no less than three translations of Mr. Murray have been produced by the Court Theatre. I hope it may not be long before an original play by him may again be produced in London under the management of Messrs. Vedrenne and Barker, or under some other management. Mr. Murray lives in an atmosphere nowadays very conducive to the dramatic genius. I noticed him the other day at the pageant in the city in which he now lives, the city of Oxford. Talking of Oxford, I was much struck with the book of the pageant, and in turning over its leaves I was deeply impressed by a dramatic episode in verse. "Here," I said to myself, "I scent a new dramatist." I turned to the title-page, and found the name of Laurence Housman. Mr. Housman is the joint author with Mr. Granville Barker himself of that charming play, *Prunella*, which produced in their first season, has again been produced during the last few weeks, and shows signs of becoming a classic. I also see here Mr. St. John Hankin, the author of two comedies produced at the Court Theatre.

He is a typical product of modernity, and the success of his witty criticisms of life is of immense encouragement to all who look for brilliant modern comedies. Mr. Hankin has not only been a pillar of the Court Theatre—he is also a champion in the fight for the freedom of the stage, and is doing doughty work for the drama generally, for which all lovers of the theatre should be grateful. The soul of the drama must have elbow room—it needs the freedom of space in which to spread its wings. Mr. Frederick Fenn is here also, the author of *The Convict on the Hearth,* produced last year at the Court Theatre. And Mr. John Galsworthy, whose play, *The Silver Box,* is, by universal consent, one of the ablest plays written in the last few years. I also see Mr. John Masefield, whose play, *The Campden Wonder,* has encouraged some people to think that we have room for a Grand Guignol Theatre in London. I see Mr. Robert Vernon Harcourt is also present this evening. I am glad that a son of a great Chancellor of the Exchequer, and a brother of a Cabinet Minister, should devote his talents to dramatic work. I have heard it said that the drama should be, or is, as potent a force in the development of a nation as the Church. Certainly Mr. Harcourt's presence today shows that the State and the theatre are becoming more closely allied. Perhaps one of these days Mr. Harcourt will persuade the Government to give us a Ministry of Fine Arts. Ladies and gentlemen, these are only some of the authors of the Court Theatre. Their presence here tonight and the sucess of so many of their plays during the past two or three years does show that there is a new development, the more encouraging and hopeful because it proceeds in so many instances from young men, in the English stage of today.

I confess that I feel a jealousy—a not ignoble jealousy, I hope—of Messrs. Vedrenne and Barker. I think I proved in years past that I was always ready to open my door to the younger generation which was knocking at it. It has always been a source of deep regret to me that the conditions of the theatre over which I now preside have precluded my devoting my wholehearted energies to the modern drama. If the palatial proportions of our building have placed certain limitations upon my efforts in this direction, it is pleasant to think that my loss has been the gain of our guests of tonight. It is impossible that every production in an undertaking of this kind should be equally successful, but I have never come away from any of these productions without a feeling that here, indeed, was an institution in which the art of the theatre was worthily striven for. If the flour with which the bread was made differed in quality, the yeast was the same—the yeast of the presiding genius, the yeast of a directing personality. There can be no doubt that the drama has advanced most hopefully during these latter years. I remember that when I first went on the stage all the characters in a play-bill (with the possible exception of a comic footman or singing chambermaid) had to be dukes or duchesses, peers or peeresses—none under an "honourable" or an occasional colonel was admitted to that select society. The drama today appeals to a wider humanity— it treats in a more philosophic spirit with the actions and the passions of mankind. The theatre is no longer the toy of fashion—intellect is the pose of the lower middle classes. I am glad to see we are so largely represented tonight. The Court Theatre has rendered a large service in holding itself proudly aloof from becoming the pander of fashion—its message is to the people at large—a healthy antidote to that spirit of snobbery which, in the opinion of many serious men, afflicts our national life, which worships at the shrine of wealth and of rank and of worldly power. It seems strange that the people of a proud nation should always be aping their inferiors.

It is right that we should thank these authors, and that we should encourage them to persist in holding up the mirror to the nature of their time. It is right also that we should encourage them to those reaches of imagination which give to humanity the idealised truth—this, the highest achievement of all art. I ask you in this toast to show your appreciation of what these authors have done. I give you the toast, "The Authors of the Court Theatre," coupled with the name of Mr. Bernard Shaw.

Mr. G. Bernard Shaw in replying, said:—

A good deal has been said here tonight as to how much our guests of the evening owe to me. My lord, ladies and gentlemen,

I assure you they owe me nothing. They are perfectly solvent. The success, such as it is, has been a perfectly genuine one. There are plenty of managements who will make a brilliant show of success if you give them a sufficiently large subsidy to spend. Vedrenne and Barker have had no subsidy. They have paid me my fees to the uttermost farthing; and they have had nothing else to pay or repay me. This does not mean that the highest theatrical art is independent of public support, moral and financial. The Court Theatre has had to cut its coat according to its cloth; and it has never really had cloth enough. But it has paid its way and made a living wage for its workers; and it has produced an effect on dramatic art and public taste in this country which is out of all proportion to the mere physical and financial bulk of its achievements.

I am glad to have the honour of speaking here for the Court Theatre authors, because if they had to answer for themselves they would be prevented from doing themselves justice by their modesty. Modesty fortunately is not in my line; and if it were I should follow the precept offered by Felix Drinkwater to Captain Brassbound, and be modest on my own account, not on theirs. As a matter of fact I am overrated as an author: most great men are. We have, I think, proved that there is in this country plenty of dramatic faculty—faculty of the highest order too—only waiting for its opportunity; and it is the supreme merit of our guests this evening that they have provided that opportunity. You may say that genius does not wait for its opportunity: it creates it. But that is not true of any particular opportunity when there are alternatives open. Men of genius will not become the slaves of the ordinary fashionable theatres when they have the alternative of writing novels. The genius of Dickens, who at first wanted to write for the theatre, was lost to it because there was no theatre available in which his art could have breathed. I have myself tried hard to tempt Mr. Wells, Mr. Kipling, Mr. Conrad, and Mr. Maurice Hewlett, to leave their safe and dignified position as masters of the art of fiction, and struggle with new difficulties and a new *technique*—though the technical difficulties are absurdly exaggerated—for the sake of redeeming the British drama from banality. But it was too much to ask.

They all knew the story of the manager who, after receiving favourably a suggestion of a play by Stevenson, drew back in disgust on learning that the author in question was not what he called *"the* Stephenson," meaning the librettist of a well-known light opera, but one Robert Louis Stevenson, of whom he had never heard. If Mr. Maurice Hewlett was persuaded at last to make an experiment at the Court Theatre, it was because he knew that Vedrenne and Barker would know his worth and respect his commanding position in literature. Without that no alliance between literature and the theatre is possible; for it is hard enough to make one reputation and conquer one eminence without having to set to again as a stranger and a beginner on the stage. If Mr. Galsworthy, after winning his spurs as one of the finest of the younger novelists, brought to the stage in *The Silver Box* that penetrating social criticism, and that charm of wonderfully fastidious and restrained art which makes me blush for the comparative blatancy of my own plays, it is because there was at last a stage for him to bring them to, and that stage was the Court stage, the creation of Vedrenne and Barker. Barker, by the way, was not, like Vedrenne, wholly disinterested in the matter, for he, too, is a Court author, and he, too, produces work whose delicacy and subtlety requires exquisite handling. It is Vedrenne's just boast that he has produced Barker. The same thing is true of all the Court authors, more or less. Mr. St. John Hankin, the Mephistopheles of the new comedy, would have been suspected by an old-fashioned manager—and suspected very justly—of laughing at him. Mr. Vernon Harcourt and Mr. Housman, whose charm is so much a charm of touch, would not have had much more chance than Mr. Henry James has had on the long-run system. Literary charm is like the bloom on fine wall-fruit: the least roughness of handling knocks it off; and in our ordinary theatres literary plays are handled much as American trunks are handled at the boat trains. Mr. Gilbert Murray has not merely translated Euripides—many fools have done that, and only knocked another nail into the coffin of a dead language—he has reincarnated Euripides and made him a living poet in our midst.

But Vedrenne and Barker made a Court author of him when no other managers dared touch him.

The difficulties of the enterprise have been labours of love, except in one unfortunately very trying respect. There has been no sort of satisfaction in the unremitting struggle with the London press, which from first to last has done what in it lay to crush the enterprise. I know this uncompromising statement will surprise some of you, because in every newspaper you see praises of Vedrenne and Barker, ecstasies over the Court Theatre acting, paragraphs about the most frequently played Court author and so forth. That has become the fashion; and the indiscriminate way in which it is done shows that it is done as a matter of fashion rather than of real appreciation. But if you turn back from this new convention to the points at which newspaper notices really help or hinder management— to the first night notices of the first productions—you will see what I mean. There you will find a chronicle of failure, a sulky protest against this new and troublesome sort of entertainment that calls for knowledge and thought instead of for the usual *clichés*. Take for example the fate of Mr. Masefield. Mr. Masefield's *Campden Wonder* is the greatest work of its kind that has been produced in an English theatre within the recollection—I had almost said within the reading—of any living critic. It has that great English literary magic of a ceaseless music of speech—of haunting repetitions that play upon the tragic themes and burn them into the imagination. Its subject is one of those perfect simplicities that only a master of drama thinks of. Greater hate hath no man than this, that he lay down his life to kill his enemy: that is the theme of the *Campden Wonder;* and a wonder it is—of literary and dramatic art. And what had the press to say? They fell on it with howls of mere Philistine discomfort, and persuaded the public that it was a dull and disgusting failure. They complained of its horror, as if Mr. Masefield had not known how to make that horror bearable, salutary, even fascinating by the enchantments of his art—as if it was not their business to face horror on the tragic stage as much as it is a soldier's business to face danger in the field. They ran away shamelessly, whining for happy endings and the like, blind and deaf to the splendid art of the thing, complaining that Mr. Masefield had upset their digestion, and the like. And what they did brutally to the *Campden Wonder* they did more or less to every other play. As we rehearsed our scenes and rejoiced in the growing interest and expectancy of our actors as they took the play in, we knew that no matter how enthusiastic our audience on the first night would be, no matter how triumphant the success of our actors, the next day—always a day of reaction at the best of times—would bring down on them all a damp cloud of grudging, petulant, ill-conditioned disparagement, suggesting to them that what they had been working so hard at was not a play at all, but a rather ridiculous experiment which was no credit to anybody connected with it. The mischief done was very considerable in the cases of new authors; and the discouragement to our actors must have had its effect, bravely as they concealed it. Now, we were all—we authors—very much indebted to our actors, and felt proportionately disgusted at the way in which they were assured that they were wasting their time on us. I should like to make my personal acknowledgements to all of them; but that is a duty reserved for a later speaker; so I will only give, as an instance, the fact that my own play, *John Bull's Other Island*, failed as completely in America without Mr. Louis Calvert as Broadbent as it succeeded here, where it was carried on his massive shoulders. The success was his, not mine: I only provided the accessories. Well, you will say: But did not the press acknowledge this? is not the play always spoken of as a masterpiece? is not Mr. Calvert's Broadbent as famous as Quin's Falstaff? Yes, it is—*now*. But turn back to the first night notices, and you will learn that the masterpiece is not a play at all, and that Mr. Calvert only did the best he could with an impossible part. It was not until *Man and Superman* followed that the wonderful qualities of *John Bull* were contrasted with the emptiness and dullness of its successor. It was not until *Major Barbara* came that the extinction of all the brilliancy that blazed through *Man and Superman* was announced. And not until *The Doctor's Dilemma* had been declared my Waterloo was it mentioned that *Major Barbara* had been my Austerlitz.

Now I want to make a suggestion to the press. I don't ask them to give up abusing me, or declaring that my plays are not plays and my characters not human beings. Not for worlds would I deprive them of the inexhaustible pleasure these paradoxes seem to give them. But I do ask them, for the sake of the actors and of Vedrenne and Barker's enterprise, to reverse the order of their attacks and their caresses. In the future, instead of abusing the new play and praising the one before, let them abuse the one before and praise the new one. Instead of saying that *The Doctor's Dilemma* shows a sad falling off from the superb achievement of *Major Barbara*, let them say that *The Doctor's Dilemma* is indeed a welcome and delightful change from the diseased trash which they had to endure last year from this most unequal author. That will satisfy their feelings just as much as the other plan, and will be really helpful to us. It is not the revivals that we want written up: the revivals can take care of themselves. Praise comes too late to help plays that have already helped themselves. If the press wishes to befriend us, let it befriend us in need, instead of throwing stones at us whilst we are struggling in the waves and pressing life-belts on us when we have swum to shore.

At the close of Mr. Shaw's speech, Mr. Frederick Whelen announced that he had been informed by the management of the Criterion Restaurant that it being after eleven o'clock, it became necessary to terminate the proceedings. The remaining toasts were therefore given without speeches. By the courtesy of Mr. Gilbert Murray, Miss Wynne-Matthison, Sir Oliver Lodge, and Mr. William Archer, the undelivered speeches are here added.

Mr. Gilbert Murray, in moving the toast of "The Players of the Court Theatre,"

Proposed, after making some remarks in answer to previous speakers to dwell upon the peculiar delicacy and sincerity of the style of acting seen at the Vedrenne-Barker performances; qualities, in his opinion, which were not to be found in equal perfection in even the best French acting. He proposed, so far as his audience would permit, to discuss, with illustrations, the effects of the profession of acting upon the human character, as compared with the far worse effects produced by all the other professions with which he had been brought in contact: to describe the peculiar artistic pleasure of conscious and vivid co-operation in the production of a beautiful thing, which belonged to the art of the stage more than to any other, and to rehearsals more than to performances: to concur with other speakers in thinking that the attainment of this spirit of co-operation was one of the great causes of the special charm of the Court performances, and to end by coupling the toast with the name of Miss Wynne Matthison, whose representations of *Andromache* and of *Electra*, by their beauty, sincerity and profound understanding, had made on him an impression which nothing could efface.

Miss Wynne-Matthison, in responding proposed to say:

Lord Lytton, ladies and gentlemen,— "The words of Mercury are harsh after the songs of Apollo"; and indeed I should feel much hesitancy in replying to the distinguished poet and scholar who has just spoken, were it not for the friendly inspiration of your sympathy and the pride I have in being called upon to represent my dear comrades, the players of the Court Theatre.

For us it was a happy choice that made Professor Murray the spokesman of this toast, for it gives us the opportunity of publicly thanking him and his brother authors for the noble and uplifting work they have entrusted to our interpretation at the Court Theatre. This is a point upon which our gratitude cannot be too strongly expressed. Our authors have fitted us out with an entirely new gallery of theatrical portraitures: freeing us from the conventional classifications which have done injustice for humanity too frequently upon the English stage, they have compelled us to turn to the study of living men and women, and have thus founded a new tradition in our national dramatic art. The gain to the actor is enormous: it means new joy, new inspiration; let us hope it may mean in the near future that we may hear no more of that silly affectation in the cheaper cynicism of the day, which would compare the art of the actor with the meaningless mimicries of the ape, but that we too may be regarded as worthily taking our share in that noble gift of imitation which consists in the heroic interpretation of the divine destinies and issues of our common human life.

And to the public and to that organised body of public opinion, the press, we owe no less a debt of gratitude. I am aware that I am here treading upon very delicate ground—the sop to Cerberus is an exceedingly difficult morsel to administer, the power of biting in three places at once presenting a rather complicated and peculiar problem; but if, on the one hand, I flinch from the possible interpretation of sycophancy, on the other I should feel criminally ungrateful—and I am sure my comrades will support me—if I were not to express how deep a sense of obligation we feel towards those stern arbiters of our fortune I have mentioned. It would be an affectation to pretend that we were less open to the blandishments of praise than the perhaps more salutary influences of blame—and we have had our share of both!—but I think we may fairly claim, taking an all-around estimate of the matter, that we have received from public and press alike a most generous share of sympathy and help, if not as much as our greed would desire, yet as is good for us. They have helped us by taking us seriously in our efforts toward the attainment of our very difficult art; they have helped us by concentrating their interest more and more upon our work, and less and less upon our domestic idiosyncrasies and picture-postcards; they have helped us, above all, by their support of the Court Theatre, its aims and objects, its enthusiasms, its principles, and the movement of which it is the embodiment and symbol.

Lastly, for that movement itself, we do indeed render our most profound and abiding thanks. And in this connection, perhaps we may be pardoned—as players of the Court Theatre —if we boast that for us, at least, the movement very much means our beloved friends and fellow-workers, Vedrenne and Barker. I say "friends and fellow-workers" advisedly, because I am bound to confess to one very serious defect in the Court Theatre system: it has imbued us with a great disrespect for dignitaries. We have found that we can get on very well without them. Messrs. Vedrenne and Barker themselves have suffered from this defect: we may admire them for their great work, we may love them for their many kindnesses, but we cannot for the lives of us regard them in their august function as employers of labour. On the contrary, they have taught us to treat them for all the world as if they were quite common working-men like ourselves! In all other respects we have nothing but praise for them: they may be very bad masters, but as servants—as servants in the cause of the actor—they do very well. At the Court Theatre there have been no rancours, no jealousies, no groans of the ill-paid and sweated in our midst; sanely and surely there has been realised among us there a very real and a very precious sense of human brotherhood and sympathy, firmly based on economic equity and artistic opportunity. We are glad to think, ladies and gentlemen, that Messrs. Vedrenne and Barker do not stand alone among London managers in this respect—the presence of Mr. Tree is a sufficient reminder of the fact—but at least we may claim for our two friends their honourable place among the very foremost ranks of all. That's why we players love them; that's why we wish them God-speed in their new enterprise; that's why we reserve our remaining thanks—last, not least— for them, their splendid work, and the many blessed opportunities we have received at their hands.

Sir Oliver Lodge, in moving the toast, "Success to the Savoy," proposed to say:—

As an outsider I am glad to be allowed to speak on this occasion, in order to express part of the debt which I and many others unconnected with the profession owe to the series of wonderfully interesting and admirably acted plays which have been produced at the Court Theatre.

And now the company is going to leave the Court, which I suppose has become—in the words of a brilliant analytical programme recently laid before a set of matinee audiences— "an abysmal void." But after all the Court was not much a locality as an idea—a state of the soul,—and migration, therefore, will be more in name than in reality; the spirit will survive the transition, and there will be a reincarnation at the Savoy, carrying with it not only a memory of the past but the full character and personality which we have known hitherto.

As to the public, however, the public certainly consists of bodies—we often speak of public bodies—and to them locality will make a considerable difference. They must be instructed as to the new place. They must learn where to go; and I am wondering whether they can obtain access to the Savoy by "Tube," so as to replace the former access by "Underground." I am not well acquainted with the approaches to the Savoy, but perhaps the landlord could usefully expend a week's rent in improving them. I hope that the artisan class may find a central position more convenient, and that arrangements can be made to prevent their having to waste time by standing in a queue. I should like them to see *Major Barbara* in especial, though no doubt it will puzzle them, as it has puzzled others, in places. That is what is so admirable about many of these plays; they give, as the Chairman has said, intellectual enjoyment, but they keep the intelligence pleasantly on the stretch all the time, and leave us at the end in a somewhat puzzled condition as to the meaning of the author and his view of the universe. It is very good for people to be puzzled, and very bad for them to think that they can understand, or that they do understand, the universe, without any mental effort. I want workmen to see *Hippolytus* also, and to realise the humanity of those old times.

It may be said that the artisan classes have not leisure enough to exert foresight and book seats beforehand; but other people are busy to, and I often feel the same difficulty. I have not seen *The Voysey Inheritance* for instance, nor *The Silver Box*, though I will make a point of seeing both when they are reincarnated; but if one goes without prevision one cannot be sure of a seat—at least not of a good seat;—for though matinée hats may have been partially abolished, people have taken to erecting their hair in a compensatory fashion, and putting things in it, which, though doubtless effective enough in a proper place, are in a theatre repulsively ugly, since they show total disregard of other people.

178 •

Another bad habit of people in the front row of a dress circle is to spoil the architect's design by leaning forward on their elbows, so as effectively to obstruct the view of the row behind. Sometimes, it is true, this does not matter; but when Mr. Charles Ricketts has designed the costumes, and when Mrs. Granville Barker is on the stage, we do not wish the picture spoilt by something irrelevant in the immediate foreground.

The fact is, going to a theatre in this country is not made as comfortable or as attractive as it might be; and the pleasure felt at receiving an invitation, from an author or a manager to a play, is due, not to the trivial circumstance of escaping the payment of a few shillings, but to the realisation that you are welcome, and that a good seat will be provided.

I have been wondering whether Mr. Vedrenne could not devise a plan whereby really interested people could subscribe a sum in advance and be entered on the books; so that, if on any particular day they found themselves able to go, they could send a short notice and be sure that there would be a good seat for them—not always the same seat of course, but a reasonable seat—somewhat on the concert plan; the price of it being debited against their deposit, without having to pay at the doors, and without being relegated to a bench at the back. I feel as if I should go more often, and send my friends more often, to a theatre where I had this sort of entrée, than I do at present when one is only a member of the general public, with no particular interest at one box office more than at another.

It is most true, as William Archer has urged, that educated people have a duty to attend and support a theatre where real plays are given; they ought to try and make it more profitable (though I am afraid it is not at present) to produce good stuff than to produce rubbish. The production of a play is a notable example of co-operation—co-operation between the dramatist, the actors, the manager, the scenic artist, the public, and the critics—and of these the public has not as yet recognised its full duty in the matter. I should like to say much about the actors; but it would take long, and others have spoken on the subject.

As to the critics, it seems to me that they often err on the side of severity; sometimes they appear to judge plays from a preconceived standard, as if they should all be moulded on one pattern. Yes, I remember that a notable critic attacked plays consciously—perhaps conscientiously—from this point of view; but I do not call such a writer a critic, I call him a missionary; and if he is understood in that sense no harm is done.

There is often a controversy as to the degree of elaboration suitable for the production of a play, but I suggest that there is room for all kinds and degrees of elaboration. When Mr. Tree gives us a gorgeous setting for *Antony and Cleopatra* I am grateful. There are some plays for which a gorgeous setting is suitable or almost necessary; there are others for which it is unnecessary or even out of place. We had a historical play at the Court where the setting needed was of the simplest character—we had in fact two—one was *A Man of Destiny*, the other was *Captain Brassbound*. I call it historical because the same sort of thing is going on in Morocco now, and Sir Harry MacLean has walked into the trap, out of which Miss Ellen Terry is not there to rescue him.

Concerning the plays produced by the leading author of the Court Theatre, I have heard many adverse opinions: seldom moderate ones. People either violently appreciate or violently condemn. I have heard him spoken of somewhat in this fashion. . . . Someone by name George Shaw—no relation I hope to anyone present—appears to be a desperate villain; he is the infamous author of a monstrous play—a play advocating mendacity—a play suppressed, I am glad to say, in America. It is called *How Mrs. Warren Lied to her Husband*—lied about her age, her income, about all the things that silly women do lie about. Sir Charles Wyndham is running a sequel to it in this very building. And then the author has the assurance to re-name the play *Candida*, because one of the characters, having stripped every rag of decency from the discussion, proceeds to tell the frozen truth. . . .*

Yes, some frozen and some burning truths are to be found in Mr. Shaw's plays: I do not say that there is nothing else.

---

*Ellipses as in the original.

He is telling society some home truths, and waking them up out of their stupid self-satisfaction, stripping them of many illusions, one of which is that things as they are are satisfactory. But as a matter of fact things on this planet are far from perfect: they can be mended; and it is our business to mend them. The first thing is to realise that they are wrong. People all over the country are waking-up to the fact—to the double fact,—first that things are wrong, second that the remedy is in our hands; and therefore I say it is an epoch of hope. The walking-up is being accomplished by literature, by the writings of some of those present, and by the stage, far more than by the pulpit. By the pulpit too, however; and "more power to the pulpit" I would say, on due occasion. But here and now the toast shall take the form, "Success to the Savoy."

Mr. William Archer, in moving a vote of thanks to the Chairman, proposed to say:—

Ladies and gentlemen, it is my agreeable duty to propose a vote of thanks to our Chairman. There is a historical, a hereditary fitness in the presence of Lord Lytton in the Chair tonight. His distinguished grandfather was one of the most ardent supporters of William Charles Macready in his gallant effort to stay the decline of the British drama, about the middle of last century. Sir Edward Lytton Bulwer, as I think he then was, even presented a play to Macready without fee or reward —none other than the dear old *Lady of Lyons*. I don't know whether Mr. Shaw has insisted on offering to Messrs. Vedrenne and Barker a like testimony of his regard; but I do know many other authors—and authoresses—who would be quite willing to emulate Sir Edward's generosity. Moreover, our Chairman's grandfather took the Chair at one of the complimentary dinners to Macready, at which he (Bulwer) recorded that "Mac looked like a baffled tyrant." I do not see that expression on the countenance of either of our guests tonight; but tyrants I am sure they are, else they would not be successful managers. Fortunately, I believe the members of their company recognise their autocracy as a beneficent one; wherefore they neither are, nor appear to be, "baffled." But the great difference between the occasion to which I refer and the present occasion is that, whereas Macready was making a gallant effort to stay the decline of the drama, Vedrenne and Barker are no less gallantly hastening, furthering, promoting, stimulating its revival. His was a losing battle, theirs is a winning battle; for the spirit of the time is on their side. We are here tonight to express to Vedrenne and Barker our gratitude for the past, our most cordial encouragement for the future; and I am sure you will agree with me in thanking Lord Lytton for lending to our little festival the distinction of a name long famous in dramatic history, and for so gracefully and eloquently serving as the spokesmen of our feelings.